CITYSPOTS
ROTTE

Thomas

WHAT'S IN YOUR GUIDEBOOK?

Independent authors Impartial up-to-date information from our travel experts who meticulously source local knowledge.

Experience Thomas Cook's 165 years in the travel industry and guidebook publishing enriches every word with expertise you can trust.

Travel know-how Contributions by thousands of staff around the globe, each one living and breathing travel.

Editors Travel-publishing professionals, pulling everything together to craft a perfect blend of words, pictures, maps and design.

You, the traveller We deliver a practical, no-nonsense approach to information, geared to how you really use it.

ABOUT THE AUTHOR

Based in Amsterdam, Pip Farquharson has been enjoying a love affair with the intoxicating Dutch capital for 15 years... while being seduced by Rotterdam on the side. She regularly contributes to leading travel guides and publications, and has consulted on programmes for the BBC, MTV, Channel 4 and Lonely Planet. In her spare time, she deejays, drinks cocktails and dreams of living somewhere sunnier.

Thomas
Cook

CITYSPOTS
ROTTERDAM

Pip Farquharson

Written by Pip Farquharson

Published by Thomas Cook Publishing
A division of Thomas Cook Tour Operations Limited
Company registration No: 1450464 England
The Thomas Cook Business Park, 9 Coningsby Road
Peterborough PE3 8SB, United Kingdom
Email: books@thomascook.com, Tel: +44 (0)1733 416477
www.thomascookpublishing.com

Produced by The Content Works Ltd
Aston Court, Kingsmead Business Park, Frederick Place
High Wycombe, Bucks HP11 1LA
www.thecontentworks.com

Series design based on an original concept by Studio 183 Limited

ISBN: 978-1-84157-923-8

First edition © 2008 Thomas Cook Publishing
Text © Thomas Cook Publishing
Maps © Thomas Cook Publishing/PCGraphics (UK) Limited
Transport map © Communicarta Limited

Series Editor: Kelly Anne Pipes
Production/DTP: Steven Collins

Printed and bound in Spain by GraphyCems

Cover photography (Cubical House) © Giovanni Simeone/4Corners Images

CONTENTS

INTRODUCING ROTTERDAM

Introduction 8

When to go 10

Renowned
  Rotterdammers 14

History 16

Lifestyle 18

Culture 20

**MAKING THE MOST OF
ROTTERDAM**

Shopping 24

Eating & drinking 26

Entertainment
  & nightlife 30

Sport & relaxation 34

Accommodation 36

The best of Rotterdam 40

Suggested itineraries...........42

Something for nothing 44

When it rains 46

On arrival 48

THE CITY OF ROTTERDAM

The Centre 58

Around Museumpark 74

Waterfront 86

OUT OF TOWN TRIPS

Amsterdam 104

Apeldoorn 116

PRACTICAL INFORMATION

Directory 128

Emergencies 138

INDEX 140

MAPS

Rotterdam city map 50

Rotterdam transport map ...54

The Centre 60

Around Museumpark 76

Waterfront 88

Amsterdam
  & Apeldoorn 106

SYMBOLS KEY

The following symbols are used throughout this book:

@ address ☎ telephone ❶ fax ⓦ website address ⓔ email
🕒 opening times Ⓝ public transport connections ❶ important

The following symbols are used on the maps:

𝒊	information office	▪	points of interest
✈	airport	○	city
✚	hospital	○	large town
🛡	police station	○	small town
🚌	bus station	═	motorway
🚆	railway station	—	main road
Ⓜ	metro	—	minor road
✝	cathedral	—	railway
❶	numbers denote featured cafés & restaurants		

Hotels and restaurants are graded by approximate price as follows:
£ budget price **££** mid-range price **£££** expensive

◗ *Historic Delfshaven*

Introduction

If Amsterdam is the *enfant terrible* of the Netherlands, then
Rotterdam is the besuited adult who has been forced to grow
up quickly – yet hasn't lost their sense of fun.

◯ *Piet Blom's* Kubuswoning *(cube houses)*

During World War II, the strategic harbour city suffered terrible devastation when German Luftwaffe planes carpet bombed the entire inner city, forcing the neutral Netherlands (which they'd invaded four days earlier), to surrender. Ironically, this one, single, horrific event was responsible for shaping the Rotterdam of today, a dynamic city which, upon first encounter, swiftly dispels any prior notions about the Netherlands being a land of clogs, windmills and quaint, gabled houses lining picturesque canals. Ambitious post-war reconstruction, when town planners were handed a *carte blanche* to rebuild Rotterdam in any style they saw fit, has turned the second-most populated city in the Netherlands into a veritable architects' playground: its metro station (resembling a flying saucer), its oddly tilted cube houses, and its iconic Erasmusbrug (Erasmus Bridge, see page 92) have made it a mecca for architecture aficionados from all over the world.

Rotterdam is where, in 1953, Europe's first pedestrianised shopping precinct (see page 24) opened, and it became the prototype for other cities in Europe and even America. The shopping area which has sprung up around it has, by the way, made Rotterdam a fantastic destination for a weekend spree.

Its massive port, which stretches around 40 km (25 miles) to the North Sea, was, for more than four decades, the largest in the world. Not only is it the driving force behind the economy of the city, but of the entire country, too. And, in turn, it's created a city of hard-working, multicultural Rotterdammers.

But, with its vibrant festivals, lively nightlife, superb art museums, eclectic clubs, bars and restaurants, Rotterdam is certainly not all work and no play...

When to go

There's no shortage of things to do in Rotterdam. Visitors pour into the city in summer, though the crisp spring and autumnal days are equally charming. Winter is an ideal time to hit the museums or engage in some retail therapy.

SEASONS & CLIMATE
Whatever time of year you go, there's one simple rule concerning Dutch weather: pack an umbrella.

ANNUAL EVENTS
For further information on festivals and events, check
ⓦ www.rotterdam.info or ⓦ www.rotterdamsuitburo.nl

January
International Film Festival Rotterdam (IFFR) A fantastic festival that screens the best independent features and documentaries from around the world. ⓦ www.filmfestivalrotterdam.com

February
ABN Amro World Tennis Tournament One of the world's largest men's indoor tennis tournaments. ⓐ Ahoy, Ahoyweg 10 ⓣ (010) 235 2469 ⓦ www.abnamrowtt.nl ⓜ Metro to Zuidplein

March
Rotterdam Museum Night Rotterdam's art galleries and museums open their doors from 20.00–02.00. ⓦ www.rotterdamsemuseumnacht.nl

April

Museum Weekend Two days of free admission to the city's museums. Ⓦ www.museumweekend.nl

Koninginnedag (Queen's Day) The notoriously boozy Dutch national holiday, with flea markets, concerts and parties. And booze. Ⓦ www.rotterdam.info

May

Ortel Dunya Festival World music, poetry and literature converge in the city's central park, **Het Park** (Ⓦ Parkhaven 20). Ⓦ www.dunya.nl

June

Concours Hippique International Officiel (CHIO) The country's largest outdoor equestrian event. Ⓐ Kralingse Bos, Kralingseweg 120 ❶ (010) 452 8900 Ⓦ www.chio.nl Ⓜ Metro to Kralingse Zoom or Voorschoterlaan; tram: 7

De Parade A terrific, olde-worlde-vibed theatre festival that takes place in Rotterdam's Museumpark. Ⓦ www.deparade.nl

July

North Sea Jazz Festival The world-famous jazz festival moved from The Hague to Rotterdam in 2006. Ⓐ Ahoy, Ahoyweg 10 ❶ (010) 235 2469 Ⓦ www.northseajazz.com Ⓜ Metro to Zuidplein

Ortel Summer Carnival Rotterdam's answer to London's Notting Hill Carnival, but rooted in Antillean culture.

August

Bavaria City Racing Rotterdam's centre transforms into a racing circuit for three days of motorsports. Ⓦ www.bavariacityracing.nl

 *The North Sea Jazz Festival is just one of Rotterdam's many music festivals*

September

Gergiev Festival A unique event centred on symphonic music, founded by Russian conductor Valery Gergiev.
 www.gergievfestival.nl

Open Monumentendag (Heritage Days) Historical buildings fling their portals open, gratis.  www.openmonumentendag.nl

R'Uitmarkt All sorts of free performances herald the new cultural season.  www.ruitmarkt.nl

De Wereld van Witte De With This festival of film, theatre, dance, music, fashion and visual arts celebrates Rotterdam's cultural epicentre.  Witte de Withstraat  www.festivalwww.nl
 Metro to Beurs or Eendrachtsplein; tram 7, 8, 20, 21, 23, 25

October
Dance Week Location-specific improv, experimental work and dance films. ⓦ www.dansweek.nl

November
Night Of The Proms Classical music meets pop classics at this concert series that's inspired by the Brits' Last Night of the Proms. ⓦ www.notp.com

December
Kerstmarkt A charming Christmas market sets up in the city's botanical gardens, Arboretum Trompenburg (see page 35). ⓦ www.trompenburg.nl

PUBLIC HOLIDAYS
New Year's Day 1 January
Good Friday 21 March 2008, 10 April 2009
Easter Sunday & Monday 23 & 24 March 2008, 12 & 13 April 2009
Koninginnedag (Queen's Day) 30 April
Ascension Day 1 May 2008, 21 May 2009
Liberation Day 5 May
Whit Sunday & Monday 11 & 12 May 2008, 31 May & 1 June 2009
Christmas Day & Boxing Day 25 & 26 December

On these days, government departments, banks, shops and even some restaurants are closed.

Renowned Rotterdammers

It's rather unfortunate that a survey taken a few years ago revealed that the majority of Rotterdammers thought Erasmus was the architect of the Erasmusbrug (Erasmus Bridge, see page 92). In fact, the early Renaissance writer, scholar and humanist Desiderius Erasmus (born in Rotterdam, in 1466), is the city's most famous figure – and the person after whom that iconic bridge is named.

His best-known work, published in 1511, is *The Praise of Folly*, a satirical attack on corruption and superstition within the church. However, it was his published collections of more than 4,000 proverbs that were the bestsellers of his day. In fact, he's the man ultimately responsible for bringing many of them into modern usage, from the old adage 'Prevention is better than cure' to 'Women: can't live with them, can't live without them'. He's even credited with introducing that charming nugget of urban slang, 'to give someone the finger' into the vocabulary.

Painter Willem de Kooning was also born in Rotterdam, in 1904. In 1926, he stowed away on a cargo ship bound for America, where, along with Jackson Pollock, he became a leading exponent of the post-war Abstract Expressionism movement. His greatest achievement came posthumously, at the end of 2006, when Sotheby's sold his painting *Untitled XXV* (1997) for a whopping £13 million, a world auction record for any post-war work. When it's not on loan, De Kooning's *Cliff of the Palisade with Hudson River* (1963) can be found at the Boijmans van Beuningen Museum (see page 78).

Architect's architect Rem Koolhaas is also a Rotterdam native. The son of Dutch writer Anton Koolhaas, he was born in 1944, and studied scriptwriting at the Netherlands Film Academy in Amsterdam (producing a screenplay which piqued the interest of Russ Meyer). He also worked as a journalist en route to becoming one of the world's most celebrated contemporary architects. His contributions to his home town include the Museumpark (see page 74) and Kunsthal (see page 79).

The famed scholar from Rotterdam, Erasmus

History

Rotterdam grew from a small fishing settlement at the lower end of a stream fen known as the Rotte (meaning 'muddy water'). Around 1270, a dam was constructed at the mouth of the Rotte to shore off what is now the River Maas ('Meuse'), and the Dutch, in typically pragmatic fashion, simply named this settlement Rotte-dam.

By 1328, when Rotterdam built its first port, the Oude Haven (Old Harbour), its early settlers were already burgeoning international traders. However it wasn't until 7 June 1340, when Count Willem IV of Holland granted it a town charter, that Rotterdam – with its population of around 2,000 – really became established. Trade and shipping prospered and, by the end of the 16th century, its population had increased ten-fold. And the expansion continued, both culturally and economically, during the 17th-century 'Golden Age' heyday of the powerful Dutch East India Company.

In 1872, De Nieuwe Waterweg ('The New Waterway'), a 10-km (6-mile) channel linking the Rhine and Maas with the North Sea, was opened. This heralded the age of mass shipping and, with the development of steam power and railways, the city expanded rapidly, well into the 20th century.

However, during the 1930s, unemployment and poverty gripped the city when the Netherlands suffered an exceptionally long depression, the knock-on effect of America's 1929 Stock Market Crash. Then, just as the city was slowly starting to recover, World War II broke out, with unimaginably horrific consequences. On 14 May 1940, four days after invading the neutral Netherlands,

ROTTE-DAM
The original dam – 400 m (1,312 ft) long and 45 m (148 ft) wide – from which Rotterdam takes its name is no longer visible, but lies several metres below the surface of the city. It runs its subterranean course along the path of what is now the Hoogstraat (High Street), ending up as many lonely meanderers do, at Rotterdam Bibliotheek (Rotterdam Library, see page 62).

Germany launched a devastating blitzkrieg ('lightening war') on Rotterdam, forcing the Netherlands to capitulate. Almost the entire city centre was flattened by bombs dropped by the Luftwaffe. Along with countless factories, cinemas, hospitals and schools, approximately 24,000 houses were destroyed; 77,000 people were made homeless, and between 800 and 900 killed. The instantaneous destruction of Rotterdam's heart was followed by five years of German occupation, during which the city's Jewish population suffered indescribable losses. On 5 May 1945, Allied forces liberated the country.

Incredibly, despite having experienced such utter devastation, the tenacious Rotterdammers soon set about rebuilding their city and restoring its economic stability. Architects created a city centre unlike any other in the Netherlands, and the port was expanded – by 1962, Rotterdam Port was the largest in the world and remained so until 2004, when it was surpassed by Shanghai. But when you encounter its vastness, you'll realise it's all just semantics, really. These days, as climate change takes hold, Rotterdam is more likely to concern itself with its sophisticated flood defence system.

Lifestyle

There's a saying that, in Rotterdam, shirts are sold with the sleeves already rolled up. Second only in population to Amsterdam, the metropolis enjoys its reputation as a no-nonsense 'working city'. But although Rotterdammers might work hard, they play hard, too, spending their money on the latest gadgets and designer clothes, dining out and partying. That's perhaps hardly surprising when the city has the youngest population in the whole of the Netherlands.

Although the Dutch are generally perceived as blond, blue-eyed giants (they're the tallest nation on earth), a trip to Rotterdam swiftly dispels such stereotypes. The city has embraced multi-culturalism and is home to many nationalities, with large Moroccan, Turkish, Surinamese and Antillean populations in particular. Similarly, despite the odd political row about the burqa, the country strives to welcome all creeds (the largest being Catholicism), though you could be forgiven for thinking the only religion practised on a Sunday was shopping.

As Dutch is not the most widely spoken language in the world, you won't be expected to use it, although it's always polite to say *dag* (hello/goodbye), and *dank u wel* (thank you very much). *Alstublieft* (please) is used both when asking for something or when you are handing someone something (as in 'here you are'). And *boer* may come in handy on occasion: the Dutch hate being called a 'farmer'.

As most people speak English fluently, it's unlikely that you'll encounter any communication difficulties. Be aware, though, that, despite being a rather reserved nation, the Dutch are quite

◆ *Dining out is a favourite pastime of the young populace of Rotterdam*

blunt in their manner of speaking. This can appear rude, especially to those used to the politeness of the Brits. Don't be offended. Instead, appreciate the fact that they get straight to the point and tell you exactly what's on their mind. In turn, don't offend them by automatically assuming that because of the country's relaxed cannabis laws they all smoke *jointjes* – they're far more likely to indulge in *appeltaart* (apple pie).

Culture

Rotterdam has a vibrant and thriving arts scene; so much so, in fact, that it hardly draws breath all year round, with a hefty daily programme of art, film, music and theatre sandwiched in between several world-class festivals. It's also home to the world-famous **Rotterdam Philharmonic Orchestra** (ⓦ www.rpho.nl). The city's other cultural treasures include the groundbreaking contemporary dance companies, **Scapino Ballet** (ⓦ www.scapinoballet.nl) and **Dance Works Rotterdam** (ⓦ www.danceworksrotterdam.nl), and **RO Theater** (ⓦ www.rotheater.nl), whose eclectic Dutch productions are never less than engaging or innovative.

If international musicians such as Pink Floyd, Coldplay or Kylie Minogue play just one gig in the Netherlands, it's likely to be at the **Ahoy** (ⓐ Ahoyweg 10 ⓣ (010) 235 2469 ⓦ www.ahoy.nl), a huge steel-centric stadium across the River Maas in the south of the city. Very occasionally, some hoary old turn might be tempted to shake a leg at Feyenoord Stadium (see page 34). For contemporary, edgier music, check out the Rotown (see page 73), which has a sophisticated programme of national and international indie bands. The leading classical music venue in town is De Doelen (see page 63), where the Rotterdam Philharmonic resides. This is the place to listen to symphonic orchestras, chamber ensembles, opera or world music.

Although Rotterdam has many diverse museums, it's those around Museumpark (see page 74) that are the real gems. An absolute must is the Boijmans van Beuningen (see page 78) for its wealth of art treasures dating from the Middle Ages. And don't miss the park's unique white villas, the Chabot Museum

🔺 *Lovers of architecture are well catered to at the NAi*

(see page 74) and Huis Sonneveld (see page 78), which were once private homes but are now open to the public. Architecture lovers could spend a whole day in the NAi (see page 80), the world's largest architecture institute; but do get out and about to see Rotterdam's stunning architecture for yourself. Most museums are closed on Mondays.

● *De Doelen is a modern venue for classical music*

Rotterdam has a massive contemporary art scene. To get your fix, head to the controversial Rem Koolhaas-designed Kunsthal (see page 79) in the Museumpark, which stages superb international exhibitions. Then wander down the adjacent Witte de Withstraat to thought-provoking institutes such as MAMA (see page 79), and TENT (see page 81). If you're in town on a Friday evening, experience the local underground scene at De Aanschouw (see page 74), possibly the smallest art gallery in the world. And be sure to pop into Roodkapje (see page 79). Photography fans should head to the Nederlands Fotomuseum (see page 96). Finally, the city has a lot of public art, including a 'Sculpture Terrace' on the Westersingel, so keep an eye out.

● *The River Maas flows through Rotterdam*

MAKING THE MOST OF
Rotterdam

Shopping

While it might not have the glamour of London or Paris, Rotterdam certainly holds its own as a prime shopping destination. The centre of the city is almost solely devoted to retail therapy and is virtually car free. Shops trade seven days a week, though only the major ones tend to open on Monday morning – but fear not: any lost shopping hours can be made up for during Friday's *koopavond* (shopping evening), when stores stay open until nine o'clock.

The central, compact shopping district, just a few minutes' walk from the station, is where you'll find all the big department stores like De Bijenkorf (see page 66) and Hema (see page 67), as well as numerous fashion outlets. Shopping here revolves around the famous Lijnbaan, Europe's first pedestrianised shopping precinct, and the adjacent Beurstraverse, an underground passage beneath the Coolsingel which the locals rather rudely call the *Koopgoot* (shopping gutter).

USEFUL SHOPPING PHRASES

How much is...?
Hoeveel kost (het)...?
Hoo-fayl kost (het)...?

Can I try this on?
Mag ik dit passen?
Makh ik dit passen?

I'm a size...
Ik heb maat...
Ik hep maat...

I'll take this one
Deze neem ik
Day-ze naym ik

BINNENROTTE MARKET

Rotterdam's vast open-air market purveys second-hand items and antiques, clothing and fresh produce, including cheese, fruit and vegetables, from more than 450 stalls. ⓐ Binnenrotteplein ⓒ 08.00–17.30 Tues, 12.00–18.00 Fri, 08.00–17.00 Sat, 12.00–17.00 Sun, closed Mon ⓝ NS/Metro to Blaak; tram 21

For upmarket fashion, dip into the numerous boutiques on the nearby Van Oldenbarneveltstraat and Karel Doormanstraat. Art lovers and those in search of cutting-edge fashion, streetwear or vintage clothes, should head to the Witte de Withstraat, Oude Binnenweg and Nieuwe Binnenweg (the latter is also home to several record shops).

An absolute must is the gorgeous Westelijk Handelsterrein (Western Trade Terrain, see page 97), for its sublime designer shops, restaurants and art galleries.

Finally, extreme shopaholics should head to the Netherlands' largest indoor shopping centre, the **Zuidplein** (ⓐ Zuidplein ⓘ (010) 481 0344 ⓦ www.zuidplein.nl), or mega-shopping complex **Alexandrium** (ⓐ Watermanweg ⓘ 0800 1598 ⓦ www.alexandrium.nl). If you can't find what you're looking for here, there is no hope for you.

For suggestions on where to spend, pick up the tourist board's handy leaflet, *8 Shopping Routes on Foot*.

Eating & drinking

It's probably safe to say that Dutch cuisine doesn't rate very highly around the world, and that's hardly surprising when the country's national dish is *hutsput*, a simple, 'working-class' veg and potato stew.

Thankfully, multicultural Rotterdam has embraced culinary traditions from all around the world. A stroll down one street alone could involve wafts of Indonesian spices, fragrances of cardamom and coconut, lemongrass-infused red curry with a hint of basil from a Thai kitchen, or Aztec and Mayan aromas from a Mexican eatery.

There's a huge array of establishments to suit every pocket. Of course, with the Dutch being the world's number-one producers of cheese, you can't leave town without trying some. But don't necessarily go for the obvious bright yellow wheel of Gouda or the red wax-coated Edam. They're actually pretty tasteless. Instead, head to the open-air Binnenrotte Market (see page 25), where you can nibble cheeses infused with nuts or herbs and spices, or local *boerenkaas* (farmer's cheese), which is often organic.

The Dutch are also world famous for their beer. Again, it would be a shame to drown in Heineken when you could sample

PRICE CATEGORIES
Ratings are based on the approximate cost of a three-course meal for one person, excluding drinks.
£ up to €20   **££** €20–30   **£££** over €30

USEFUL DINING PHRASES

I'd like a table for (two), please
Ik wil graag een tafel voor (twee) personen
Ik vill khraakh an taa-fel for (tway) persoanen

Could I have the bill, please?
Mag ik de rekening alstublieft?
Mag ik de ray-ken-ing als-too-bleeft?

I am vegetarian
Ik eet vegetarisch
Ik ate veg-ay-tar-eesch

Where is the toilet, please?
Waar is het toilet, alstublieft?
Vaar is het twa-let, als-too-bleeft?

something local, so head to **De Pelgrim** (ⓐ Aelbrechtskolk 12
ⓣ (010) 477 1189 ⓦ www.pelgrimbier.nl) in the Delfshaven.
The only working brewery in the city, it produces three standard
beers and a variety of seasonal brews from within a charming
building that dates from 1580. If you're visiting in the winter,
be sure to try the lethal Winterbier, with its 10.5 per cent alcohol
content. Thankfully, you can soak up some of its effects at the
adjoining restaurant. Tours of the brewery are given every day
(apart from Monday), for groups of eight.

Plenty of choice for dining al fresco

FRIES WITH MAYO

Ironically – and thanks to Quentin Tarantino – the food most associated with the Dutch is probably their chunky Belgian-style French fries, served drowning in mayonnaise (a little Dutch touch made famous in *Pulp Fiction*). Hot and crispy on the outside and mushy on the inside, *patatjes* are also served with *oorlogsaus* (war sauce), which sees the mayonnaise do battle with peanut sauce. For the best in town, head to **Bram Ladage** (ⓦ www.ladage.nl) who have various outlets, including the Binnenwegplein 24, Kruisplein 155 and Hoogstraat 172a in the heart of the shopping district. They've been renowned for their 'haute cuisine' fries far beyond the city's boundaries since the mid-1960s.

If you don't mind being a little 'touristy', and want to combine dining with a trip along the River Maas, Rotterdam has a number of 'sailing restaurants' which offer a variety of all-you-can-eat buffet cruises. The **China Boat** (ⓣ (010) 436 1911 ⓦ www.chinaboat.nl) and **Pancake Boat** (ⓣ (010) 436 7295 ⓦ www.pannenkoekenboot.nl) depart from the foot of the Euromast (see page 90). **The Tapas Boat** (ⓣ (010) 436 7295 ⓦ www.detapasboot.nl) and **Indian Curry Boat** (ⓣ (010) 436 7295 ⓦ www.rederijthor.nl) leave from opposite Haringvliet 100 in the Oude Haven (Old Harbour). Hint: the names of the boats give an indication of what food to expect.

Tipping isn't compulsory. However, if you feel the service has been good, add approximately ten per cent of the bill or just leave some spare change.

Entertainment & nightlife

Metropolitan and innovative, Rotterdam's nightlife is constantly evolving, largely due to a predominantly young population and visionary entrepreneurs who are investing in new bars and clubs. And, although it might not have the cool factor that Amsterdam, Berlin and Paris enjoy, that's probably because Rotterdammers see their city as one of Europe's best kept secrets – and want to keep it that way.

When it comes to bars, head to those along the waterfront, within picturesque old harbours or with views over the River Maas (whose vivid illumination makes it spectacular at night). Generally speaking, bars stay open until midnight or 01.00 during the week, and 02.00 on Friday or Saturday. However, there are a few late-night drinking joints including the Bootleg DJ Café (see page 72), which opens until 06.00 from Thursday to Sunday and can also be a great opportunity to see new local and international talent.

The city's major clubs convene in the centre, with a few gems along the waterfront. However, it's worth heading off the beaten track to **Herr Zimmerman** (ⓐ Van Helmontstraat 17–23 ⓦ www.herrzimmerman.eu). A former meat factory, just beyond the Delfshaven, it opens every Saturday for an edgy slice of avant-garde Berlin in the form of underground electro.

Most clubs open from Thursday to Sunday night and generally stay open until 05.00. As public transport stops running around 00.30 and doesn't resume until around 05.30, you may have to

---

◗ *Have a great night's entertainment at Holland Casino*

rely on taxis or 'BOB' night buses (see page 53) to get you back to your hotel.

To find out what's on in Rotterdam, pick up a free copy of the weekly *NL10 magazine*, distributed in bars, restaurants and supermarkets throughout the city, or check it out on Ⓦ www.mijnnl.nl. Although it's in Dutch, the listings (especially for music, clubs and film) are fairly decipherable.

⬤ *The ultra-sleek Nieuwe Luxor theatre*

Located within the Rotterdam Library, **Rotterdams Uitburo** (ⓐ Hoogstraat 110 ⓣ (010) 240 0166 ⓦ www.rotterdamsuitburo.nl) is a one-stop shop for tickets to all cultural events.

You can also buy tickets for events (and attractions) at the VVV Rotterdam Store (see page 136). For information on more underground and less commercial events, pop in to Rotterdam Use-it (see page 136). And, of course, watch out for glossy flyers in bars, record stores, clothing and skate shops.

When it comes to something more high-brow, Rotterdam has ample choice. However, although it has many theatres, including the stunning **Nieuwe Luxor** (ⓐ Posthumalaan 1 ⓦ www.luxortheater.nl), plays and musicals are mostly performed in Dutch. (They even change the lyrics of English-language musicals to Dutch, usually with disastrous results.) However, the Rotterdamse Schouwburg (Rotterdam Theatre, see page 64) often stages English-language plays, cabaret or comedy from visiting companies.

Dance rarely encounters language barriers, and if you want to see some excellent choreography, check out contemporary companies Scapino Ballet Rotterdam (see page 20) and Dance Works Rotterdam (see page 20).

For classical music and opera, as well as occasional world music and jazz, make for De Doelen (see page 63). Be warned, though, that whether it's a Russian or Italian opera, the subtitles will be in Dutch. Similarly, foreign-language films are usually screened with Dutch subtitles.

Finally, if you feel like a flutter, dress to impress and head to **Holland Casino** (ⓐ Weena 624 ⓣ (010) 206 8206 ⓦ www.hollandcasino.nl), which is open every night until 03.00.

Sport & relaxation

Football is the most popular spectator sport in Rotterdam, with support divided between Sparta, the oldest professional football team in the Netherlands, and the mightier Feyenoord Rotterdam – Ajax's great rival!

SPECTATOR SPORTS

Feyenoord Stadium Nicknamed the *kakkerlakken* (cockroaches) and 100 years old in 2008, Feyenoord Rotterdam may have wobbled recently, but their supporters remain fiercely loyal. However, when fans went on the rampage in Nancy during the 2006 UEFA Cup Final, the team was banned for the rest of the season. Be warned: when Feyenoord score, they burst into *I Will Survive*. The 1937 stadium, nicknamed *De Kuip* (The Tub), holds 50,000 and hosted the 2002 UEFA Cup Final, which the cockroaches thankfully won. ⓐ Van Zandvlietplein 3 ⓣ (010) 292 3888 ⓦ www.feyenoord.com ⓝ Tram: 23 (also tram 29 on match days)

PARTICIPATION SPORTS

Abseiling Every weekend from May to September, adrenaline junkies can abseil or rope slide 100 m (328 ft) down the Euromast (see page 90). Groups of 20 can do it all year round. ⓐ Parkhaven 20 ⓣ (015) 256 5662 ⓦ www.abseilen.nl ⓝ Tram: 8
Bicycle rental Go Dutch and hire your wheels from **Use-it** ⓐ Schaatsbaan 41–45 ⓣ (010) 240 9158 ⓦ www.use-it.info ⓛ 09.00–18.00 Tues–Sun, mid-May–June, mid-Sept; 09.00–18.00 July & Aug; 09.00–17.00 Tues–Sat, mid-Sept–mid-May ⓝ NS/Metro to Centraal Station; tram: 4, 7, 8, 20, 21, 23, 25

⬤ *All aboard the water luge at Tropicana*

Swimming A huge glass structure houses subtropical indoor water park, **Tropicana**. It has whirlpools, slides, lagoons and a constant temperature of 30°C (86 °F). ⓐ Maasboulevard 100 ⓣ (010) 402 0700 ⓦ www.tropicana.nl ⓛ 10.00–22.00 Mon–Fri, 10.00–20.00 Sat & Sun ⓜ Metro to Oostplein; tram: 21. Admission charge

RELAXATION

Arboretum Trompenburg This beautiful botanical garden dating back to 1820 never fails to provide an antidote to fast-paced city life. ⓐ Honingerdijk 86 ⓣ (010) 233 0166 ⓦ www.trompenburg.nl ⓛ 09.00–17.00 Mon–Fri, 10.00–16.00 Sat & Sun, Apr–Oct; 12.00–16.00 Nov–Mar ⓜ Tram 21. Admission charge

Accommodation

You'll be spoilt for choice when it comes to accommodation in Rotterdam, whether it's the nostalgic Hotel New York (see page 38), a stylish suite high up in the Euromast tower (see page 38), or one of the city's sublime new boutique or designer hotels. You can even sleep on board historic cruise ship SS *Rotterdam* (see page 93), or within one of Piet Blom's famous cube houses (Kijk-Kubus, see page 91). But do book in advance, especially during the summer months.

HOTELS

Maritime Hotel £ Despite its dull façade and basic rooms, this 3-star hotel has a prime location on the River Maas. ❷ Willemskade 13 ❶ (010) 411 9260 ❺ (010) 411 9262 ❼ www.maritimehotel.nl ❽ Metro to Leuvehaven; tram: 7, 20, 23, 25

Hotel Bazar £–££ A charming, Middle-Eastern bolthole in the heart of Rotterdam's artistic quarter, above the Bazar restaurant (see page 84). ❸ Witte de Withstraat 16 ❶ (010) 206 5151 ❺ (010) 206 5159 ❼ www.bazarrotterdam.nl ❽ Metro to Beurs; tram: 8, 20, 21, 23, 25

> ### PRICE CATEGORIES
> Based on the average price of a standard room for two people for one night.
> £ up to €100   ££ €100–200   £££ over €200

A Small Hotel ££ A luxury boutique hotel with just six rooms on Rotterdam's coolest cultural street. ⓐ Witte de Withstraat 94 ⓣ (010) 414 0303 ⓦ www.asmallhotel.nl ⓝ Tram: 7

Golden Tulip Rotterdam-Centre ££ Next to the Erasmus Bridge, this contemporary hotel has spectacular views over the water. *Pièce de résistance* is the indoor pool. ⓐ Leuvehaven 80 ⓣ (010) 413 4139 ⓕ (010) 413 3222 ⓦ www.goldentuliprotterdamcentre.com ⓔ reservationsrotterdam@goldentuliphotelinntel.com ⓝ Metro to Leuvehaven; tram: 7, 20, 23, 25

ART Hotel Rotterdam ££–£££ As the name suggests, this 4–star hotel across the River Maas is a must for creative types.

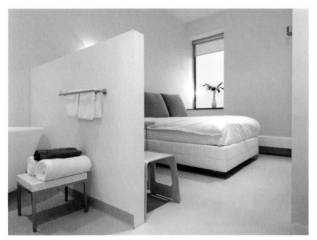

△ *The clean lines of the mega-minimalist Stroom hotel*

ⓐ Mijnsherenlaan 9 ⓣ (010) 279 4111 ⓕ (010) 279 4112
ⓦ www.arthotelrotterdam.com ⓝ Metro to Maashaven; tram: 2

Bilderberg Parkhotel ££–£££ Dating from 1922, Rotterdam's
oldest hotel is located on the edge of the Museumpark and has
a charming courtyard garden. ⓐ Westersingel 70 ⓣ (010) 436 3611
ⓕ (010) 436 4212 ⓦ www.bilderberg.nl ⓝ Tram: 7

Hotel New York ££–£££ A decadent, art nouveau hotel within
the former head office of the Holland America-Line (HAL)
that's a must for a nostalgic experience. ⓐ Koninginnenhoofd 1
ⓣ (010) 439 0500 ⓦ www.hotelnewyork.nl ⓝ Metro to
Wilhelminaplein; tram: 20, 23, 25

Stroom ££–£££ In the trendy Lloydkwartier, this fantastic designer
hotel is big on beds and baths! It has a cool roof terrace and
some rooms have video phone facilities. ⓐ Lloydstraat 1
ⓣ (010) 221 4060 ⓦ www.stroomrotterdam.nl ⓝ Tram: 8

Westin Rotterdam £££ The city's only 5-star hotel is geared towards
business travellers and located just opposite Centraal Station in
the futuristic Millennium Tower. ⓐ Weena 686 ⓣ (010) 430 2000
ⓦ www.westin.nl ⓔ rotterdam.westin@westin.com ⓝ NS/Metro
to Centraal Station; tram: 4, 7, 8, 20, 21, 23, 25

APARTMENTS
Euromast Heaven & Stars £££ For a unique experience and
stunning vista, rent one of the two stylish (non-smoking) suites

in the Euromast (see page 90). ⓐ Parkhaven 20 ❶ (010) 241 1788 ⓦ www.euromast.nl ⓝ Tram: 8

BOATS

De Clipper £ A cheap-and-cheerful, family-run hostel on a charming boat in one of the city's old harbours. ⓐ Across from Scheepsmakershaven 26 ❶ (06) 38 35 39 43 ⓝ NS/Metro to Blaak; metro to Leuvehaven; tram: 8, 20, 21, 23, 25

HOSTELS & CAMPSITES

ROOM Rotterdam £ An arty backpackers' hostel within the Scheepvaartkwartier that has 16 individually themed rooms, ranging from two-person to ten-person. ⓐ Van Vollenhovenstraat 62 ❶ (010) 282 7277 ⓦ www.roomrotterdam.nl ⓝ Metro to Leuvehaven; tram: 7, 8

Stadscamping Rotterdam £ Just ten minutes by bus from the centre, this campsite is pitch perfect whether you have a tent, caravan or campervan. You can also rent one of their cosy two- or four-person wooden cabins. ⓐ Kanaalweg 84 ❶ (010) 415 9772 ⓦ www.stadscamping-rotterdam.nl ⓝ Bus: 33

Stayokay Rotterdam £ A short walk from the Museumpark, this large hostel has a laundry, kitchen, internet facilities and a beautiful garden at the back. You can also rent bikes here, and it's open 24 hours a day. ⓐ Rochussenstraat 107–109 ❶ (010) 436 5763 ⓦ www.stayokay.com ⓝ Metro to Dijkzigt; tram: 4

THE BEST OF ROTTERDAM

Rotterdam is a fairly compact city, so it's easy to fit in the key sights, even on a flying visit.

TOP 10 ATTRACTIONS

- **High tea at Hotel New York** Experience a bygone era of trans-Atlantic travel, and do it in style (see page 97)

- **Abseil or rope slide down the Euromast** A fantastic way to experience this unique landmark, and just think of the holiday snaps (see page 90)

- **Go to the zoo** The historic Diergaarde Blijdorp is a great day out, especially its underwater shark tunnel. Just don't eyeball the gorillas (see page 133)

- **Take a trip down the River Maas** The city from the water is stunning – particularly at night. Take a boat tour or hop on the amphibious bus (see page 93)

- **Culture fix** Head straight for the Museumpark and Witte de Withstraat for the city's premier art museums and galleries (see page 74)

- **Kijk-Kubus** Piet Blom's wonky cube houses confirm Rotterdam's reputation as an architects' playground (see page 91)

- **Sample the local beer** De Pelgrim brewery in the historic Delfshaven has barrels of charm (see page 27)

- **Shop till you drop** With its compact shopping centre, gorgeous designer shops and super shopping centres, a spot of retail therapy is a must (see page 24)

- **Strand aan de Maas** If the temperature soars, chill out at the city's fantastic, centrally located urban beach (see page 93)

- **Go on board the SS *Rotterdam*** Witness the grandeur of the largest passenger ship ever built in the Netherlands (see page 93)

⬥ *The riverside café in front of the Hotel New York*

Suggested itineraries

HALF-DAY: ROTTERDAM IN A HURRY
See all the city's major sights – including a trip on the River Maas – on an amphibious bus with Splashtours (see page 93). Then pop into Dudok (see page 70) for some of its famous apple pie.

1 DAY: TIME TO SEE A LITTLE MORE
Head to the Museumpark (see page 74) where all the city's major art museums converge, then wander down 'cultural street' Witte de Withstraat. Lunch at Bazar (see page 84), then take a water taxi from Leuvehaven to Hotel New York (see page 97) for high tea.

2–3 DAYS: TIME TO SEE MUCH MORE
Follow the recommendations above, but also visit the historic Delfshaven (see page 90), scale the Euromast (see page 90) and check out the Oceanium at Diergaarde Blijdorp (see page 133). Don't, of course, forget to experience some of the city's nightlife (see page 30) and shopping (see page 24).

LONGER: ENJOYING ROTTERDAM TO THE FULL
Take a boat downstream to the iconic 17th-century Kinderdijk windmills, the fascinating Europoort or the Netherlands' impressive flood defence system, the Delta Works. Do visit the historic town of Delft, made famous in *Girl with a Pearl Earring*, and renowned for its Delft Blue pottery. And if you're here mid-March to mid-May, the Keukenhof bulb fields 50 km (31 miles) away are a must.

● *The fields of windmills at Kinderdijk*

Something for nothing

Those who believe devoutly that the best things in life are free might just have come to the right place, because when it comes to freebies, Rotterdam has a lot of rich pickings.

🔵 *Boijmans van Beuningen is the city's top museum and completely free*

Every Wednesday, the city's premier museum, Boijmans van Beuningen (see page 78), has free admission. That's right: it won't cost you one cent to admire Breughel's magnum opus, *Tower of Babel*, or visit the only museum in the Netherlands that has paintings by Dalí and Magritte in its permanent collection.

And, if you're in town in April, most of the city's museums open their doors with either free or reduced entrance during Museum Weekend (see page 11). True, it can be busy, but if it coincides with one of the first hot spells of the year – as it has in the past – most Rotterdammers will be beach bound. Similarly, Open Monumentendag (Heritage Days, see page 12) takes place in September, when historical or unusual buildings (many not usually accessible to the public) open their doors for free for one weekend. And don't miss the R'Uitmarkt at the beginning of September (see page 12), when an abundance of free-entry performances, previewing the city's new cultural season, take place on and around the Schouwburgplein.

During the summer the city has a plethora of free-entry festivals, culminating with September's epic Wereldhavendagen (World Harbour Days), when the city's maritime past and present come to life all around the harbour.

And, of course, if it's fine weather, you can throw together a picnic and head to the city's central park, Het Park or waterfront beach, Strand aan de Maas (see page 93).

Finally, if you have children in tow, you can keep them entertained with free shows of puppetry (featuring the occasional live dog!) at the **Poppentheater** (Ⓦ www.poppentheater.nl). They take place on the Binnenwegplein between 13.30 and 15.30 every Wednesday, Saturday and Sunday from May to September.

When it rains

Rain is probably a given in Rotterdam, whose climate is as temperamental as it is temperate. However, it needn't put a dampener on your visit.

In fact, dark clouds looming on the horizon could provide you with the perfect excuse to head indoors for some retail therapy. You could start by browsing the upmarket fashion and design stores within gentrified warehouse complex, Westelijk Handelsterrein (see page 97). Or head downtown to the city's major department store, De Bijenkorf (see page 66) and nearby underground shopping passage, the Beurstraverse (see page 24). Thoughtfully, the architect Pi de Bruin added huge glass canopies on either side of this 'shopping gutter', in anticipation of rain stopping play. Alternatively, you could simply hole up for the day in the country's largest indoor shopping centre, Zuidplein (see page 25), or shopping emporium Alexandrium (see page 25).

Of course, rain also provides the perfect opportunity to spend hours perusing the city's fantastic museums, without feeling guilty about missing out on any good weather.

Although a damp day is probably not the best time to scale the Euromast (see page 90) if you want a decent view, it doesn't mean you have to stop sightseeing. The amphibious Splashtours bus (see page 93) will ensure you're kept dry – not only when you're viewing the city's sights but when you're cruising along the River Maas – without having to leave your seat. Spido tour boats are also covered, although do bear in mind that the grey skyline of a rainy Rotterdam does dull some of the city's usual shine.

When it rains, you can always go on the Spido

You could also head to Rotterdam's enormous public library, Bibliotheek Rotterdam (see page 62) and curl up with a good book (there are plenty of English titles), check your emails on the free internet terminals or just browse through the day's foreign-language newspapers.

If, however, the rain does end up making you cold and miserable, buy a swimsuit and head to the heat of subtropical indoor water park, Tropicana (see page 35).

On arrival

TIME DIFFERENCE

Rotterdam is on European Standard Time, one hour ahead of London. Daylight saving time applies, with clocks going forward one hour on the last Sunday in March and back one hour on the last Sunday in October.

ARRIVING

By air

Rotterdam Airport (☎ (010) 446 3444 ⓦ www.rotterdam-airport.nl) is 8 km (5 miles) northwest of the city centre. Bus 33 (☎ 0800 6061) connects to Rotterdam Centraal Station, leaving every 10 minutes. Taxis (☎ (010) 462 6060) can be found in front of arrivals. Fares are around €25 per journey, which usually takes 10–15 minutes, depending on traffic.

Schiphol Airport (☎ 0900 0141 ⓦ www.schiphol.nl) is approximately 65 km (40 miles) northeast of Rotterdam. The railway station is located directly below the airport and trains run directly to Rotterdam, approximately every 30 minutes. Journey time takes around 45 minutes.

By rail

The main railway station is **Rotterdam Centraal Station** (ⓐ Stationsplein 1 ☎ 0900 1475). The old building was demolished at the end of 2007 to make room for a stunning new version on the same site, and Dutch pragmatism has meant minimal disruption.
Wizzl National Ticket Office ⓦ www.ns.nl ⏰ 07.00–21.00 Mon–Fri, 08.00–21.00 Sat, 09.00–21.00 Sun

IF YOU GET LOST, TRY...

Do you speak English?
Spreekt u Engels?
Spraykt-oo Eng-els?

Is this the way to...?
Is dit de weg naar...?
Is dit de vekh naar...?

Could you point it out on the map, please?
Kunt u het op de kaart aanwijzen, alstublieft?
Kunt oo het op de kaart aan-wayezen, als-too-bleeft?

NS International Ticket Office ☎ 0900 9296
ⓦ www.nsinternational.nl ⏰ 07.00–20.30 Mon–Sat,
09.00–20.30 Sun

By road
Information and tickets for buses can be bought at **RET Verkoop
& Informatiepunt** (ⓐ Stationsplein ☎ 0800 6061 ⓦ www.ret.nl),
right by Centraal Station (see page 48).

Parking can be a challenge: meters no longer take coins
but use a *chipkaart* (smart card) system, and not all take credit
cards. Although multi-storey car parks do accept notes, coins
and credit cards, your best bet might be to head to the cheaper
P+R (Park + Ride) at Alexander (Exit 16 on the A20). For more
information on parking phone ☎ 0800 1545 or visit
ⓦ www.rotterdam.nl/parking

International Eurolines coaches stop at Kruisplein, outside
Centraal Station.

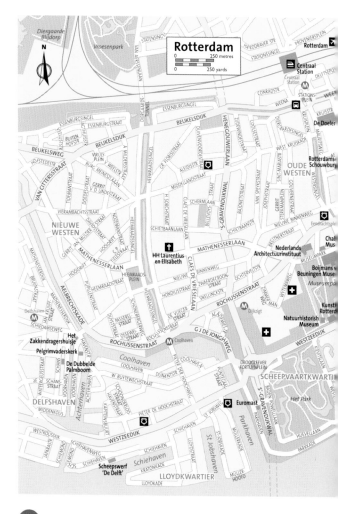

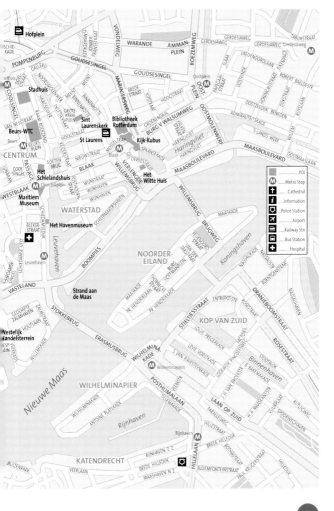

FINDING YOUR FEET

The city is so easy and pleasant to get used to that any unfamiliarity will soon disperse. However long you're in Rotterdam, it's worth buying a Rotterdam Welcome Card. Costing €5, it comes with a city map and a vouchers giving discounts to attractions, museums, shops, restaurants and clubs.

ORIENTATION

Take the Millennium Tower by Centraal Station (see page 48) as your northern navigation point and the River Maas as your southern point. To the west is the Euromast (see page 90), and to the east is the red steel Willemsbrug (Willems Bridge). Most of the area you will be exploring will be roughly within these points.

● *Willemsbrug is the red bridge to the east*

For architecture tours of the city contact **ArchiGuides** (ⓐ Conradstraat 6 ❶ (010) 433 2231 ⓦ www.rotterdam-guides.nl). **Rotterdam ByCycle** (ⓐ Conradstraat 6 ❶ (010) 465 2228 ⓦ www.rotterdambycycle.nl) offer guided cycle tours of the city. Additionally, the tourist office (see page 136), produces various free brochures of walking routes, including one detailing eight different shopping routes and one mapping out the city's art and architecture. They can also be downloaded (in PDF format) from ⓦ www.rotterdam.info

GETTING AROUND

Rotterdam has an efficient, good-value public transport system. You're more likely to take a tram or the metro than a bus, but remember that water taxis are a great (if, perhaps, expensive) way of getting around the harbour areas.

RET runs the public transport system in the Rotterdam area. Trams, buses and the metro all use the same ticket system, the OV-chipkaart (PT smart card). However, the easiest option is to buy a one-hour, one-day, two-day or three-day ticket which you can stamp yourself in the trams or at metro stations (and hand to the driver to stamp on buses). These are not valid on 'BOB' night buses: you'll have to buy a new ticket from the driver. For more information on tickets or timetables, call the RET transport line (see page 49).

Buses, trams and the metro start running every day around 05.30 and end around 00.30. After that, 'BOB' night buses take over, running from 01.00–04.30 during the week and from 01.10–06.30 at weekends. There are seven tram lines and two metro lines. Metro Erasmuslijn runs north to south, from Centraal Station to

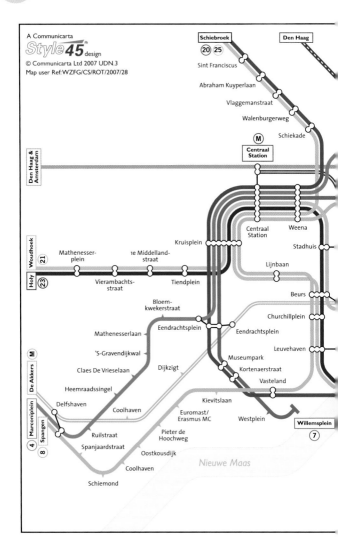

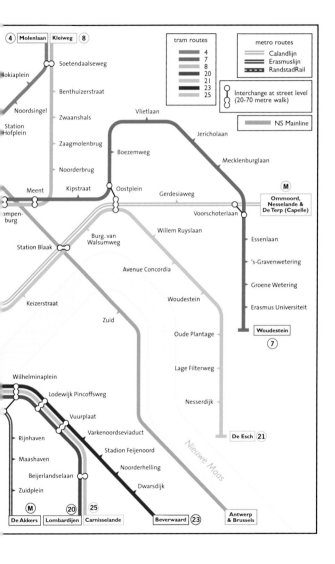

Spijkenisse. Metro Calandlijn runs east to west, from Spijkenisse to three destinations: Capelle a/d Ijssel, Onmoord and Nesselande.

There are 24-hour taxi ranks at Centraal Station. Taxis can also be hailed on the street, if the sign on the roof is illuminated. Try **Rotterdam Taxi Centrale (RTC)** (❶ (010) 462 6060) or **St Job Taxi** (❶ (010) 425 7000).

You can also opt to explore the city in a 'tourist taxi'. A one-hour tour costs around €60 (maximum three persons), and a two-hour harbour tour costs around €120 (maximum six persons). Contact **Rho Delta Events BV** (❶ (010) 292 7464).

Rotterdam has a superb water taxi network, **Water Taxi Rotterdam** (❶ (010) 403 0303 ❿ www.watertaxirotterdam.nl ❹ 07.00–24.00, until 01.00 Fri & Sat and from 09.00 Sat & Sun). There are two types of taxi – the classic wooden Hotel New York launches and the super-fast Maas Taxis.

Spido (❷ Departure point: Willemsplein 85 ❶ (010) 275 9988 ❿ www.spido.nl ❷ Metro to Leuvehaven; tram: 20, 23, 25) offer 75-minute harbour tours all year round, as well as a variety of longer tours in July and August.

CAR HIRE

All major car hire firms are based at Rotterdam Airport (see page 48). Additionally, many have offices in Rotterdam. Those near Centraal Station include **Hertz** (❷ Weena 699 ❶ (010) 404 6088 ❿ www.hertz.nl) and **Europcar** (❷ Walenburghof 17 ❶ (010) 465 6400 ❿ www.europcar.nl).

❶ *The buildings above the pier of Wilhelminahoofd*

THE CITY OF
Rotterdam

The Centre

Rotterdam's modern centre serves as both the business district
– it's where you'll find the town hall and trade centre – and the
shopping district, with its compact, largely pedestrianised retail
area. There also plenty of bars and restaurants here, although
if you want to avoid the crowds and tourist traps, head out of
the centre towards the parks and waterfront.

SIGHTS & ATTRACTIONS

Beurs-WTC

The low-rise, 1941 Beurs (Stock Exchange) by J F Staal was extended
in 1987 by a modern green tower, designed by Rob van Erk, to house
the World Trade Centre. This is the heart of Rotterdam's business
world. ⓐ Beursplein 37 ⓞ (010) 405 4444 ⓦ www.wtcrotterdam.nl
ⓝ Metro to Beurs; tram: 8, 20, 21, 23, 25

Desiderius Erasmus Statue

The oldest statue in Rotterdam (a robed man reading from an
enormous book) captures the city's most famous native perfectly
(see page 14). It was made in 1622 by Hendrick de Keyser.
ⓐ Grotekerkplein ⓝ Metro to Beurs; tram: 8, 20, 21, 23, 25

Sint Laurenskerk (St Lauren's Church)

Building on this church (sometimes known as the Great Church)
began in 1449 and took on its present form around 1523. It's the
only Late Gothic building in Rotterdam to have (just about)
survived World War II, indeed its rebuilding became symbolic

○ The heart of Rotterdam's business world, Beurs-WTC

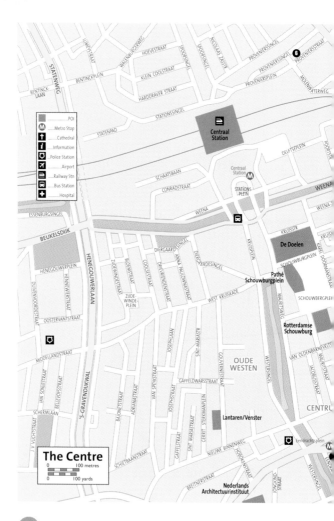

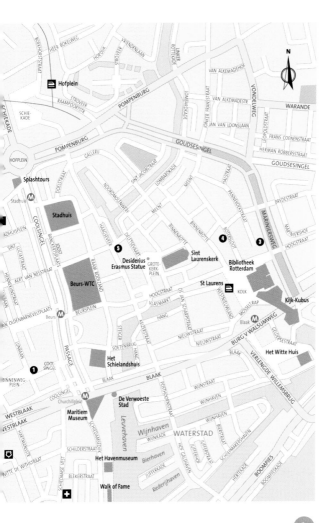

of that of the city. Concerts and other cultural events are regularly held here and, every Saturday from May to September, you can climb the 300 steps to the top of its 63-m-high (207 ft) tower (€2.50). ❷ Grotekerkplein 27 ❶ (010) 413 1494 ❿ www.laurenskerk rotterdam.nl ❻ 10.00–16.00 Tues–Sat, closed Sun & Mon ❿ Metro to Beurs; tram: 8, 20, 21, 23, 25

Stadhuis (City Hall)

Completed in 1920, this impressive neo-Renaissance building on the Coolsingel was designed by Henri Evers. ❷ Coolsingel 40

BIBLIOTHEEK ROTTERDAM (ROTTERDAM LIBRARY)

Designed by renowned local architects Van den Broek & Bakeman, this enormous public library resembles the Pompidou Centre in Paris; indeed, the huge yellow pipes on the exterior have earned it the nickname 'vacuum cleaner'. It houses more than one million books and the biggest recorded music collection in Europe. The icing on the library's cultural cake is its massive Erasmus Collection, a trove of documentation about the city's leading man of letters (see page 14). As well as free internet facilities and a café-restaurant with a terrace, it also houses the Rotterdams Uitburo ticket office (see page 33). ❷ Hoogstraat 110 ❶ (010) 281 6114 ❿ www.bibliotheek.rotterdam.nl ❻ 13.00–20.00 Mon, 10.00–20.00 Tues–Fri, 10.00–17.00 Sat, 13.00–17.00 Sun, closed Mon ❿ NS/Metro to Blaak; tram: 21

(010) 417 9111 www.rotterdam.nl Metro to Stadhuis; tram: 21, 23

Station Blaak

This underground station, which serves both trains and the metro, was designed by H C H Reijnders and resembles a flying saucer, although locals have nicknamed it 'the kettle', 'the manhole cover' and the 'transparent pancake'. Blaak 11 NS/Metro to Blaak

Het Witte Huis (The White House)

In its day, this ten-storey building was the pride of Rotterdam. The ambitious art nouveau-style building was not only the Netherlands' first skyscraper, but Europe's, too. It looks like somewhere The Addams Family might have lived.
Gelderse Kade 1 NS/Metro to Blaak; tram: 21

CULTURE

De Doelen

Its predecessor perished in World War II, but, just over 20 years later, a new, 1960s-style concert venue arose. It's home to the Rotterdam Philharmonic and has a hefty classical music programme, peppered with jazz and world music concerts.
Schouwburgplein 50 (010) 217 1717 www.dedoelen.nl
NS/Metro to Centraal Station; tram: 4, 7, 8, 20, 21, 23, 25

Lantaren/Venster

The L/V screens arthouse films daily in its four cinemas. It also has two auditoriums in which off-beat music, dance and theatre are programmed from September to May. Gouvernestraat 133 (010) 277 2277 www.lantaren-venster.nl Box Office 13.00–22.00 Tram: 4

Pathé Schouwburgplein

Within walking distance of Centraal Station, this modern, seven-screen cinema shows all the latest blockbusters. Schouwburgplein 101 0900 1458 www.pathe.nl NS/Metro to Centraal Station; tram: 4, 7, 8, 20, 21, 23, 25

Rotterdamse Schouwburg (Rotterdam Theatre)

The Rotterdam Theatre squeezes in more than 500 performances annually of highbrow theatre, dance and opera, including a fairly substantial international programme. In fact, the entire month of September is dedicated to international performances. The three kinetic sculptures on the façade are by George Rickey and move in the wind. Schouwburgplein 25 (010) 411 8110 www.rotterdamseschouwburg.nl Tram: 4, 7, 8, 20, 25

Het Schielandshuis

Built in the style of Dutch classicism with baroque details, the Schielandhuis is the only surviving building in the city centre from the 'Golden Age'. It now houses the city's historical museum. Napoleon stayed here when he visited Rotterdam in 1811. Korte Hoogstraat 31 (010) 217 6767 www.schielandshuis.nl 11.00–17.00 Tues–Sun, closed Mon Metro to Beurs; tram: 1, 8, 20, 23, 25. Admission charge

▶ *The Pathé Schouwburgplein cinema complex*

RETAIL THERAPY

The city centre is a shopaholic's paradise that triggers a child in a sweetshop reaction. It's probably best avoided on Friday evenings and weekends if you're not keen on crowds.

Bags & The City Bag fetishists need look no further than the exclusive collection found here, alongside stylish shoes and other accessories. ⓐ Van Oldenbarneveltstraat 97 ⓣ (010) 213 6688 ⓦ www.bagsandthecity.nl ⓛ 10.00–18.00 Tues–Thur, 10.00–21.00 Fri, 10.00–17.30 Sat, 13.00–17.00 Sun, closed Mon Ⓝ Tram: 8, 20, 25

De Bijenkorf The 'Beehive' is probably the closest thing Rotterdam has to Harrods. It has a great household goods department and both designer and own-label clothes, plus jewellery, cosmetics and other accessories. The 'Chill Out' department is the place to head for funky club- and street-wear. ⓐ Coolsingel 105 ⓣ 0900 0919 ⓦ www.bijenkorf.nl ⓛ 11.00–18.00 Mon, 09.30–18.00 Tues–Thur & Sat, 09.30–21.00 Fri, 12.00–18.00 Sun Ⓝ Metro to Beurs; tram: 8, 20, 21, 23, 25

Coccinelle Trendy mums can stock up on DKNY, Dior and D&G for their offspring here. ⓐ Plaza 20 ⓣ (010) 414 1184 ⓦ www.coccinelle.nl ⓛ 11.00–18.00 Mon, 10.00–18.00 Tues–Thur, 10.00–21.00 Fri, 10.00–17.30 Sat, 12.00–17.00 Sun Ⓝ NS/Metro to Centraal Station; tram: 4, 7, 8, 20, 21, 23, 25

Crumpler Funky messenger and laptop bags, plus backpacks and other luggage from this Australian brand. ⓐ Nieuwe Binnenweg 1

 (010) 225 1370 www.crumpler.nl 11.00–18.00 Tues–Fri,
11.00–17.00 Sat, 13.00–17.00 Sun, closed Mon Metro to
Eendrachtsplein; tram; 4

De Groene Passage 'The Green Passage' is an environmentally
friendly shopping centre. If it's organic, new age and/or fair-trade,
you'll find it here. When you're all shopped out, rest your feet at
the pleasant 'Bio-café'. Mariniersweg 9–33 (010) 233 1933
 08.00–20.00 Mon–Fri, 08.00–18.00 Sat, closed Sun
 Tram: 7, 8; bus; 48

Gsus Heavens Playground Creativity, total freedom and an
environmental conscience are at the heart of this world-famous
Dutch clothing brand. Oude Binnenweg 65 (010) 412 8020
 www.g-sus.com 12.00–18.00 Mon, 10.00–18.00 Tues–Thur,
Sat, 10.00–21.00 Fri, 12.00–17.00 Sun Metro to Eendrachtsplein;
tram; 4, 7

Hema Something of an institution, this Dutch department
store purveys reasonably priced, no-nonsense electrical goods,
household items and food. Beursplein 2 (010) 282 9900
 www.hema.nl 11.00–18.00 Mon, 09.00–18.00 Tues–Thur
& Sat, 09.00–21.00 Fri, 12.00–17.30 Sun Metro to Beurs;
tram: 8, 20, 21, 23, 25

Selexyz Donner A quarter of a million books are stocked on ten
floors of this answer to any bibliophile's prayer. Put your feet
up mid-ogle at Bagels & Beans (see page 69). Lijnbaan 150
 (010) 413 2070 www.selexyz.nl 11.00–18.00 Mon,

09.30–18.00 Tues–Thur, 09.30–21.00 Fri, 09.30–17.00 Sat, 12.00–17.00 Sun ⓝ Metro to Beurs; tram: 8, 20, 21, 23, 25

Shoebaloo Stunningly presented men's and women's shoes by all the usual suspects: Gucci, Dior, Prada, Fendi, Miu Miu and Alexander McQueen. ⓐ Kruiskade 57c ⓣ (010) 280 7337 ⓦ www.shoebaloo.nl ⓒ 12.00–18.00 Mon, 10.00–18.00 Tues–Thur & Sat, 10.00–21.00 Fri, 13.00–18.00 Sun ⓝ Metro to Stadhuis; tram: 21, 23

Studio Hergebruik Artists here create intriguing functional art from recycled materials. ⓐ Coolsingel 53 ⓣ (010) 413 3660

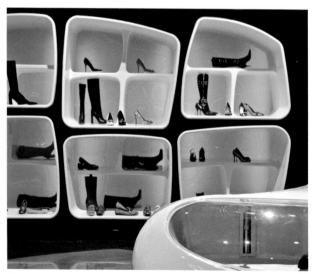

🔻 *Take your pick at Shoebaloo*

ⓦ www.studiohergebruik.nl ⓘ 12.00–18.00 Wed–Sat, 13.00–17.00 Sun, closed Mon & Tues ⓝ Metro to Stadhuis; tram: 21, 23

Van Dijk Stylish and individual high-end women's clothing by the likes of Rick Owens and Paul Smith can be found at the store of the 'Fashion Queen of Rotterdam', Wendela Van Dijk, as well as her own brand pieces. Her second shop, at Van Oldebarneveltstraat 146, specialises in French designer Isabel Marant. ⓐ Van Oldenbarneveltstraat 105 ⓘ (010) 411 2644 ⓛ 13.00–18.00 Mon, 10.00–18.00 Tues–Thur & Sat, 10.00–21.00 Fri, 13.00–17.00 Sun ⓝ Tram: 8, 20, 25

Zero10 Rotterdam's first concept fashion store carries labels such as Sacha Lannoye, Dolce & Gabbana, Alexander McQueen and Diesel. The top floor is dedicated to an Aveda hair and beauty salon. The terrace of ground-floor café Simply Bread is a great pitstop for organic food, fair-trade coffee and a spot of people-watching. ⓐ Oude Binnenweg 122 ⓘ (010) 270 9795 ⓦ www.zero10.nl ⓛ 10.00–18.00 Mon–Wed & Sat, 10.00–20.00 Thur & Fri, 12.00–18.00 Sun ⓝ Metro to Eendrachtsplein; tram: 21

TAKING A BREAK

Bagels & Beans £ ❶ Up on the fifth floor of Selexyz Donner book store (see page 67), this café, which sells fresh American-style bagels and cakes, has an enormous roof terrace. ⓐ Lijnbaan 150 ⓘ (010) 240 0738 ⓦ www.bagelsbeans.nl ⓛ 11.00–18.00 Mon, 09.30–18.00 Tues–Thur, 09.30–21.00 Fri, 09.30–17.00 Sat, 12.00–17.00 Sun ⓝ Metro to Beurs; tram: 8, 20, 21, 23, 25

Orange Café £ Award-winning Dutch restaurant chain 'La Place' is on the ground floor of this hi-tech store of mobile phone giant Orange, and is great for fast and fresh food in a buzzing environment. ⓐ Orange Flagship Store, Lijnbaan 54 ⓣ (010) 270 9795 ⓦ www.orangeflagshipstore.nl ⓛ 12.00–18.30 Mon, 09.30–18.00 Tues–Thur, 09.30–21.00 Fri, 09.30–18.00 Sat, 11.30–17.30 Sun ⓝ Metro to Stadhuis; tram: 21, 23

Proef £ This unique restaurant grew around an experimental 'food design' laboratory where every aspect of eating is explored as an art form, from the scent, colour and sound of the food, to the atmosphere, ingredients and way it's served. ⓐ Mariniersweg 259/Pannekoekstraat 120 ⓣ (010) 280 7297 ⓦ www.proefrotterdam.nl ⓛ 08.00–17.30 Tues–Sat, 10.00–17.30 Sun, closed Mon ⓝ Tram: 7, 8; bus: 48

Urban Espresso Bar £ The best coffees in town, delicious sandwiches and cakes to enjoy on the terrace or in the confines of the suburban video lounge in the basement. ⓐ Botersloot 44a ⓣ (010) 213 0768 ⓦ www.urbanespressobar.nl ⓛ 09.00–17.30 Tues–Sat, 11.00–17.00 Sun, closed Mon ⓝ NS/Metro to Blaak; tram: 21; bus: 48

AFTER DARK

RESTAURANTS
Dudok ££ This classic grand café is famous for its apple pie and is a popular meeting spot. ⓐ Meent 88 ⓣ (010) 433 3102

🔺 *Stop in for* appeltaart *at Dudok*

🔘 www.dudok.nl 🕐 08.00–24.00 Mon–Fri, 08.00–01.00 Sat, 10.00–23.00 Sun 🔘 Metro to Beurs or Stadhuis; tram: 8, 20, 21, 23, 25

Blue Mekong ££–£££ ❻ Just behind Centraal Station, this authentic Thai restaurant is an absolute gem and specialises in seven-, nine- and eleven-dish 'rice tables'. ❸ Proveniersstraat 29a ❶ (010) 466 0439 🔘 www.blue-mekong.nl 🕐 18.00–23.00 Thur–Sat, closed Sun–Wed 🔘 NS/Metro to Centraal Station; tram: 4, 7, 8, 20, 21, 23, 25 ❶ Reservations are a must

De Engel £££ ❼ Chef of this elegant establishment, Herman den Blijker, is a Dutch TV celeb. He uses only the freshest, highest-quality ingredients to produce fine French cuisine. ⓐ Eendrachtsweg 19 ⓣ (010) 413 8256 ⓦ www.engelgroep.com ⓛ 12.00–14.00, 18.00–22.00 Mon–Fri, 18.00–22.00 Sat, closed Sun ⓝ Metro to Eendrachtsplein; tram: 7

BARS & CLUBS

Bootleg DJ Café Young and established local and international DJs mix it up at this late-opening creative hotspot. ⓐ Mauritsweg 33 ⓦ www.bootlegdjcafe.com ⓛ 20.00–02.00 Wed, 20.00–06.00 Thur–Sat, closed Sun–Tues ⓝ Tram: 4, 7, 8, 20, 25

Catwalk Located in a 53-m-long (174 ft) former pedestrian subway, this is one of the city's coolest clubs. ⓐ Weena Zuid 33 ⓦ www.catwalkrotterdam.com ⓛ 23.00–04.00 Thur, 23.00–05.00 Fri & Sat, closed Sun–Wed ⓝ NS/Metro to Centraal Station; tram: 4, 7, 8, 20, 21, 23, 25

Dizzy Hugely popular, this jazz café was established more than 30 years ago. Every Tuesday evening, and occasionally other nights too, there are free live performances by Dutch and international musicians, while DJs mix up the jazz on Saturday evenings. The kitchen produces delicious meals (try the 'Chocolate Slut' dessert), and has special vegetarian and children's menus. ⓐ 's-Gravendijkwal 127–129 ⓣ (010) 477 3014 ⓦ www.dizzy.nl ⓛ 12.00–01.00 Mon–Thur, 12.00–02.00 Fri & Sat, 12.00–24.00 Sun ⓝ Metro to Dijkzigt; tram: 4

EXIT A great little club with regular live music and everything from electronica to drum'n'bass and indie parties.

ⓐ Mauritsstraat 173 ⓣ (010) 413 7500 ⓦ www.exit.nl
ⓛ 20.00–02.00 Wed & Thur, Sat & Sun, 16.00–02.00 Fri,
closed Mon & Tues ⓝ Metro to Beurs; tram: 8, 20, 25

Hollywood Music Hall If you don't mind crowds, you'll be
spoilt for choice: there are seven clubs under one roof, each with
different music, ranging from R&B to house. ⓐ Delftsestraat 15
ⓣ (010) 411 4958 ⓦ www.hmh.nl ⓛ 23.00–05.00 Thur, 22.00–05.00
Sat, closed Sun–Wed & Fri ⓝ NS/Metro to Centraal Station;
tram: 4, 7, 8, 20, 21, 23, 25

Off_Corso This converted cinema attracts hip party people
with its eclectic club nights, including inspired gay parties.
ⓐ Kruiskade 22 ⓣ (010) 411 3897 ⓦ www.off-corso.nl ⓛ 23.00–05.00
Thur–Sat, closed Sun–Wed ⓝ Metro to Stadhuis; tram: 4, 7, 8, 20,
21, 23, 25 ⓘ Occasionally open Wed & Sun

Rotown Popular with a young, alternative crowd, this small venue
puts on club nights and concerts. ⓐ Nieuwe Binnenweg 17–19
ⓣ (010) 436 2669 ⓦ www.rotown.nl ⓛ 11.00–02.00 Mon–Wed,
Sun, 11.00–03.00 Thur, 11.00–04.00 Fri & Sat ⓝ Metro to
Eendrachtsplein; tram: 4, 7

Thalia Lounge This plush lounge club was once a cinema
and has five levels, including VIP areas, a champagne
corner and cocktails galore. ⓐ Kruiskade 31 ⓣ (010) 214 2547
ⓦ www.thalialounge.nl ⓛ 23.00–05.00 Fri & Sat, closed
Sun–Thur ⓝ Metro to Stadhuis; tram: 4, 7, 8, 20, 21, 23, 25

Around Museumpark

The urban garden of the Museumpark and Witte De Withstraat
form the cultural centre of Rotterdam and are home to the city's
leading art museums. The Witte De Withstraat is crammed with
art galleries, shops, cafés and restaurants and, like the Museumpark,
provides an escape from the bustle of the nearby centre.

SIGHTS & ATTRACTIONS

Skatepark Westblaak

Located on a traffic island is this huge skatepark, where skaters
and boarders perform impressive stunts. It's free, and you can
also rent equipment. ⓐ Westblaak 107 ⓣ (010) 280 9370
ⓦ www.westblaak.com ⓛ 12.00–22.00 Mon–Fri, 12.00–19.30
Sat & Sun ⓜ Metro to Eendrachtsplein; tram: 4, 7

CULTURE

De Aanschouw/8ob

Something of a *vitrine* attached to the outside of De Schouw
bar, its main attraction is that new artists present their work
for the week every Friday evening from 20.30. ⓐ De Schouw,
Witte de Withstraat 8ob ⓣ (06) 41 40 09 27 ⓦ www.aanschouw.nl
ⓜ Metro to Eendrachtsplein; tram: 7

Chabot Museum

A white villa, originally built as a private house, that's now home
to a collection of work by Dutch expressionist painter/sculptor

⬥ The Chabot Museum by night

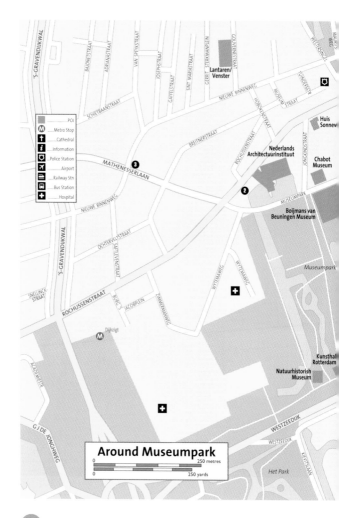

Around Museumpark

0 ————————— 250 metres

0 ————————— 250 yards

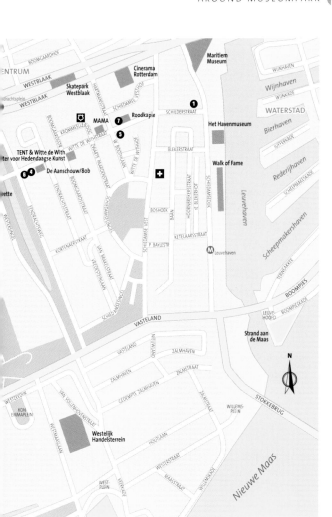

BOIJMANS VAN BEUNINGEN MUSEUM

Rotterdam's leading art museum is an undiluted treat. Its enormous collection covers the whole card, right the way back to the Renaissance superstars. Highlights include Breughel's *The Tower of Babel* (1563) and Rembrandt's touching *Titus at his Desk* (1655), alongside works by Degas, Picasso, Rubens, Magritte, Dalí and Van Gogh. The museum also stages innovative exhibitions of contemporary work.
ⓐ Museumpark 18–20 ⓣ (010) 441 9400 ⓦ www.boijmans.nl ⓛ 11.00–17.00 Tues–Sun, closed Mon ⓜ Metro to Eendrachtsplein; tram: 7. Admission charge

Henk Chabot. ⓐ Museumpark 11 ⓣ (010) 436 3713
ⓦ www.chabotmuseum.nl ⓛ 11.00–16.30 Tues–Fri, 11.00–17.00 Sat, 11.00–17.00 Sun, closed Mon ⓜ Metro to Eendrachtsplein; tram: 4, 7. Admission charge

Cinerama Rotterdam

A fabulous seven-screen cinema dating from 1960, with a busy daily schedule made up of both independent and mainstream films. ⓐ Westblaak 18 ⓣ (010) 411 5300 ⓦ www.cineramabios.nl ⓜ Metro to Beurs; tram 21. Admission charge

Huis Sonneveld

This 'white villa', designed by Brinkman and Van der Vlugt, is one of the best examples of Dutch functionalism. Its interior has been completely restored to its original 1930s glory.

ⓐ Jongkindstraat 12 ⓣ (010) 440 1200 ⓦ www.nai.nl
ⓛ 10.00–17.00 Tues–Sat, 11.00–17.00 Sun, closed Mon
ⓝ Metro to Eendrachtsplein; tram: 4, 7. Admission charge
(included with ticket to NAi) ⓘ guided tours must be
reserved at least two weeks in advance

Kunsthal Rotterdam
This striking exhibition hall, designed by Rem Koolhaas,
takes a playful, experimental approach to exhibition
planning, resulting in a diverse programme. ⓐ Westzeedijk 341
ⓣ (010) 440 0301 ⓦ www.kunsthal.nl ⓛ 10.00–17.00 Tues–Sat,
11.00–17.00 Sun, closed Mon ⓝ Tram: 7, 8. Admission charge

MAMA
Although this visual arts and cultural organisation's
obsession with things 'yoof' and edgy occasionally leads
it into self-parody, it is undeniably a launch-pad for young,
emerging artists. ⓐ Witte de Withstraat 29–31 ⓣ (010) 433 0695
ⓦ www.mamamedia.nl ⓛ 13.00–18.00 Wed–Sun, closed Mon
& Tues ⓝ Metro to Beurs; tram: 7, 8, 20, 21, 23, 25

Roodkapje
A constantly metamorphosing space offering all types
of contemporary underground art, complemented by
occasional performances, debates, lectures and artists'
dinners. ⓐ Witte de Withstraat 13 ⓣ (010) 243 9800
ⓦ www.roodkapje.org ⓛ 11.00–18.00 Wed–Sat,
12.00–17.00 Sun, closed Mon & Tues ⓝ Metro to Beurs;
tram: 8, 20, 21, 23, 25

⬤ *Natuurhistorish Museum*

Natuurhistorish Museum

A 15-m-long (49 ft) skeleton of a sperm whale takes pride of place, among stuffed birds and animals, butterflies, shells and fossils at the city's natural history museum. ⊜ Westzeedijk 345 ⊕ (010) 436 4222 ⓦ www.nmr.nl ⌚ 10.00–17.00 Tues–Sun, 11.00–17.00 Mon Ⓝ Tram: 7, 8. Admission charge

Nederlands Architectuurinstituut (NAi)

The NAi is the largest architecture museum in the world. Its four exhibition spaces offer an overview of the history of architecture and current developments. ⊜ Museumpark 25 ⊕ (010) 440 1200 ⓦ www.nai.nl ⌚ 10.00–17.00 Tues–Sat, 11.00–17.00 Sun, closed Mon Ⓝ Metro to Eendrachtsplein; tram: 4, 7. Admission charge

TENT

On the ground floor of the Witte de With Centrum voor Hedendaagse Kunst (see below), this centre for the visual arts (from video to performance) exhibits Rotterdam-centric art within a broad context. ⓐ Witte de Withstraat 50 (ground floor) ⓣ (010) 413 5498 ⓦ www.tentrotterdam.nl ⓛ 11.00–18.00 Tues–Sun, closed Mon ⓜ Metro to Beurs; tram: 7, 8, 20, 21, 23, 25. Admission charge

Witte de With Centrum voor Hedendaagse Kunst (Centre for Comtemporary Arts)

High art meets pop culture at this contemporary art centre which stages high-profile exhibitions of work by international artists. ⓐ Witte de Withstraat 50 (2nd & 3rd Floor) ⓣ (010) 411 0144 ⓦ www.wdw.nl ⓛ 11.00–18.00 Tues–Sun, closed Mon ⓜ Metro to Beurs; tram: 7, 8, 20, 21, 23, 25. Admission charge

RETAIL THERAPY

The artistic Witte de Withstraat is the area's main shopping street, where you can dip in and out of designer shops.

Betsy Palmer A treasure trove of unique and stylish shoes, including the Dutch Betsy Palmer label. ⓐ Witte de Withstraat 9 ⓣ (010) 413 5737 ⓦ www.betsypalmer.com ⓛ 13.00–18.00 Mon, 10.00–18.00 Tues–Thur, 10.00–21.00 Fri & Sat, 13.00–17.00 Sun ⓜ Metro to Beurs; tram: 8, 20, 21, 23, 25

Ecce Contemporary furniture and home accessories created by both Dutch and international designers. ⓐ Witte de Withstraat

17a–19a ☎ (010) 413 9770 ⓦ www.galerie-ecce.nl ⏰ 11.00–18.00
Tues–Thur & Sat, 11.00–19.00 Fri, 13.00–18.00 Sun, closed Mon
Ⓝ Metro to Beurs; tram: 8, 20, 21, 23, 25

Left Just opposite Skatepark Westblaak (see page 74), this skaters'
paradise has it all: boards, t-shirts, sneakers and magazines.
ⓐ Westblaak 28–30 ☎ (010) 414 5777 ⓦ www.left.nl ⏰ 10.00–18.00
Mon–Thur, 10.00–21.00 Fri, 10.00–17.30 Sat, 10.00–17.00 Sun
Ⓝ Metro to Beurs; tram: 8, 20, 21, 23, 25

Marlies Dekkers The main store of Rotterdam's famous fashion
designer. Her innovative lingerie – inspired by poetry, literature,
visual arts and film – is sold all over the world. ⓐ Witte de
Withstraat 2 ☎ (010) 280 9184 ⓦ www.marliesdekkers.com
⏰ 12.00–18.00 Mon, 10.00–18.00 Tues–Sat, 12.00–17.00 Sun
Ⓝ Metro to Beurs; tram: 8, 20, 21, 23, 25

Nieuwe Ontwerpers The minimalist 'New Designers' store stocks
work by students from the country's most prestigious fashion
institutes. You can also find original pieces by the three owners
– Henck Koers, Dick van de Vlies and Maartje Versluijs. ⓐ William
Boothlaan 13a ☎ (010) 212 4150 ⓦ www.nieuweontwerpers.nl
⏰ 12.00–18.00 Wed–Sat, 14.00–18.00 Sun, closed Mon & Tues
Ⓝ Metro to Beurs; tram: 8, 20, 21, 23, 25

TAKING A BREAK

Bagel Bakery £ ❶ American-style sweet and savoury bagels,
salads, fresh juices and other delicious deli fare served in spacious,

clean surroundings. ⓐ Schilderstraat 57a–59a ⓣ (010) 412 1560
ⓛ 09.00–21.00 Tues–Thur, 09.00–22.00 Fri & Sat, 10.00–21.00
Sun, closed Mon ⓜ Metro to Leuvehaven; tram: 8, 20, 21, 23, 25

Café Coenen £–££ ❷ Situated alongside the NAi (see page 80),
this café, named after the NAi's architect, has a beautiful view
over the Museumpark and a delightful terrace in warm weather.
Ideal for simple soups, salads and sandwiches, or a longer graze
on its daily changing menu. ⓐ Museumpark 35 ⓣ (010) 436 1952
ⓦ www.cafecoenen.nl ⓛ 10.00–23.00 Mon–Fri, 12.00–20.00 Sat
& Sun ⓜ Metro to Eendrachtsplein; tram: 4, 7

Wester Paviljoen £–££ ❸ Patronised by media folk and those
with a cultural bent, this informal grand café is housed in a
charming former pavilion dating from 1888. It's hugely popular
all day long for breakfast, lunch and dinner and has one of the
city's busiest terraces. ⓐ Nieuwe Binnenweg 136 ⓣ (010) 436 2645
ⓦ www.westerpaviljoen.nl ⓛ 08.00–01.00 Mon–Thur, 08.00–02.00
Fri, 09.00–02.00 Sat, 09.00–01.00 Sun ⓜ Tram: 4

AFTER DARK

RESTAURANTS
Mister Noodle £ ❹ A small, modern restaurant dedicated to
Vietnamese specialities, which it serves from an open kitchen.
Good value for money. ⓐ Witte de Withstraat 14a ⓣ (06) 549 4499
ⓦ www.misternoodle.nl ⓛ 16.00–23.00 ⓜ Metro to Beurs;
tram: 8, 20, 21, 23, 25

Bazar £–££ ❺ A perennial favourite, this informal, Eastern-style restaurant serves a fantastic choice of delicious North African, Iranian and Turkish food for breakfast, lunch or dinner. It's especially great for vegetarians. ⓐ Witte de Withstraat 16 ❶ (010) 206 5151 ⓦ www.bazarrotterdam.nl ⓛ 08.00–01.00 Mon–Thur, 08.00–02.00 Fri, 09.00–02.00 Sat, 09.00–24.00 Sun ⓝ Metro to Beurs; tram: 8, 20, 21, 23, 25

Toko94 ££ ❻ Creole home-style cooking meets Western techniques at this hip, Asian, fusion bar-restaurant. ⓐ Witte de Withstraat 94b ❶ (010) 240 0479 ⓦ www.toko94.com ⓛ 17.00–01.00 Tues–Thur & Sun, 17.00–02.00 Fri & Sat, closed Mon ⓝ Metro to Eendrachtsplein; tram: 7

Oliva £££ ❼ A bright and spacious restaurant with exceptional Italian cuisine prepared from an open kitchen using fresh, wholesome ingredients. Every first Sunday of the month (Oct–May), the restaurant opens from 12.00 for a 'tasting' lunch of eight dishes, accompanied by wine. ⓐ Witte de Withstraat 15a ❶ (010) 412 1413 ⓦ www.restaurantolivia.nl ⓛ 18.00–22.00 ⓝ Metro to Beurs; tram: 8, 20, 21, 23, 25

BARS & CLUBS

DP96 Adjacent to Toko94 (see above), this spacious cocktail bar attracts an internationally minded, discerning clientèle. DJs regularly spin, and huge cushions adorn its pavement terrace. ⓐ Witte de Withstraat 96 ❶ (06) 19 35 48 53 ⓦ www.dp96.hyves.nl ⓛ 13.00–01.00 Sun–Thur, 13.00–02.00 Fri & Sat ⓝ Metro to Eendrachtsplein; tram: 7

Gay Palace Rotterdam's main gay club occupies four floors and gets packed with men and women over the weekend. If the DJ puts on *YMCA* or *High Energy*, just go with the flow... ⓐ Schiedamsesingel ⓣ (010) 412 3234 ⓦ www.gay-palace.nl ⓛ 23.00–05.00 Fri, 23.00–05.30 Sat, closed Sun–Thur ⓜ Metro to Leuvehaven; tram: 7, 8

◗ *Outdoor dining at the popular Bazar*

Waterfront

Rotterdam's waterfront district is dotted with tiny harbours, each with their own character. The picturesque Leuvehaven, Oude Haven (Old Harbour) and the adjoining quays to the east of the Erasmus Bridge are full of historic clippers, barges, cranes and port equipment.

West of the Erasmus Bridge, the chic Scheepvaartkwartier (Shipping Quarter) stretches as far as the Euromast and includes Rotterdam's central park, Het Park. Remnants of the area's former maritime grandeur are still evident in its monumental buildings and leafy avenues.

Beyond, is the gentrified Lloydkwartier (Lloyd Quarter), a prime example of the city's inspired redevelopment of former harbour and industrial areas – and where the city's creative industry has converged. Just beyond here is the charming Delfshaven, one of the oldest surviving districts of Rotterdam.

Across the River Maas, dissected by the Erasmus Bridge, is the Kop van Zuid, also known as 'Manhattan on the Maas'. Its contrasting historic and contemporary architecture provide a stunning skyline. West of the bridge is the Wilhelminapier, where the renovated buildings of the Holland-America Line (HAL) steamship company are located. It was from here that emigrants set sail to New York

The Euromast is a shining beacon towering above Rotterdam

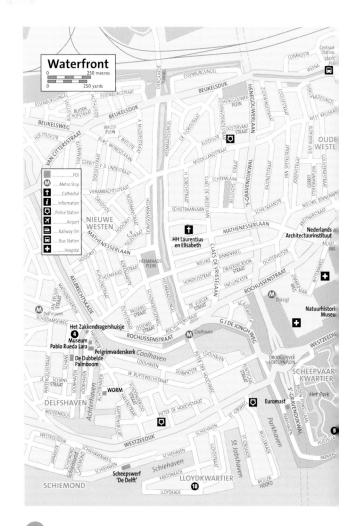

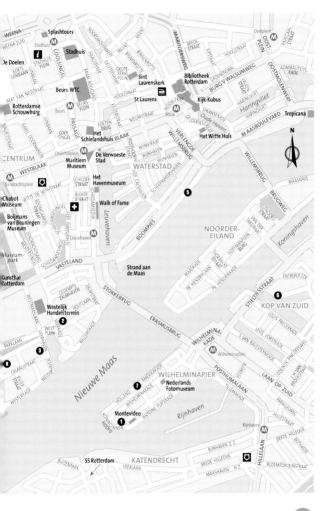

in their droves. Today's modern cruise terminal dwarfs these historic buildings. The 152-m-high (499 ft) skyscraper crowned with a large 'M' is Montevideo, the tallest residential building in the Netherlands. While the building with the almost unnerving slanting façade (the head office of telecoms giant KPN) is the creation of Italian architect Renzo Piano (the visionary genius behind Paris's Pompidou Centre and Berlin's Potsdamer Platz).

Although well served by public transport, water taxis are by far the best way to get a feel for this whole area – and experience the immensity of the Erasmus Bridge from the river.

SIGHTS & ATTRACTIONS

Delfshaven

With a history dating back to 1389, this harbour was fortunate to survive the wartime bombardment that devastated much of Rotterdam. It was originally the old port of the medieval city of Delft 15 km (9 miles) away and many of the buildings date from the 1600s. This is the spot from where, in 1620, the Pilgrim Fathers embarked on their journey to America (via Plymouth).
Ⓝ Metro to Delfshaven; tram: 4, 8

Euromast

Within 'Het Park' (The Park), and resembling a ship's mast (complete with bridge and crow's nest), the 185-m-high (607 ft) Euromast opened in 1960. Take the 'Euroscoop' (a rotating elevator) to the top for spectacular views across the city and, on a clear day, the North Sea. For information on spending the night here,

see page 38. ⓐ Parkhaven 20 ⓣ (010) 436 4811 ⓦ www.euromast.nl
ⓛ 09.30–23.00 Apr–Sept; 10.00–23.00 Oct–June ⓝ Tram: 8.
Admission charge

Kijk-Kubus (Show Cube)

A veritable testament to Rotterdam's reputation as 'an architects'
playground' is Piet Blom's cluster of 39 cube houses – all tilted and
seemingly balancing on the tip of one corner. No. 70 is open to
visitors. ⓐ Overblaak 70 ⓣ (010) 414 2285 ⓦ www.kubuswoning.nl
ⓛ 11.00–17.00 Mar–Dec; 11.00–17.00 Sat & Sun, Jan & Feb
ⓝ NS/Metro to Blaak; tram: 21. Admission charge

Pelgrimvaderskerk (Pilgrim Fathers Church)

Towering over the Delfshaven is the Pilgrim Fathers Church,
which dates from 1417. In the Eben Haëzer house at the back,
there are prints and documents about the Pilgrim Fathers,
including a passenger list of the *Mayflower*. ⓐ Aelbrechtskolk 20
ⓣ (010) 477 4156 ⓦ www.pelgrimvaderskerk.nl ⓛ 13.00–16.00
Sat ⓝ Metro to Delfshaven; tram: 4, 8

Scheepswerf 'De Delft'

In 1797, at the Battle of Camperdown (Camperduin), the English
fleet sunk the pride of the Dutch fleet, an 18th-century battleship
called *De Delft*. A replica of the ship is being built at this shipyard
and visitors can take a behind-the-scenes look at the reconstruction.
ⓐ Schiehaven 15 ⓣ (010) 276 0115 ⓦ www.dedelft.nl ⓛ 10.00–16.00
Tues–Fri, 11.00–17.00 Sat & Sun, closed Mon ⓝ Tram: 8.
Admission charge

ERASMUSBRUG (ERASMUS BRIDGE)

This stunning, asymmetric cable bridge, which spans the River Maas connecting north and south Rotterdam, was designed by Ben van Berkel and is the city's number-one sightseeing icon. 'The Swan' or 'The Harp', as it is nicknamed by locals on account of its sweeping grace, featured in the closing scenes of Jackie Chan's movie *Who Am I?*. Ⓜ Metro to Leuvehaven or Wilhelminaplein; tram: 20, 23, 25

🔺 *Erasmusbrug spans the River Maas*

Splashtours

An environmentally friendly amphibious bus takes you past the city's major sights before you don lifejackets and goggles and splash into the River Maas. ⓐ Departure point: VVV Rotterdam Store, Coolsingel 5 ⓣ (010) 436 9491 ⓦ www.splashtours.nl ⓛ 12.30, 14.00, 15.30, 17.00 Wed-Sun, Apr–June, Sept & Oct; 11.00, 12.30, 14.00, 15.30, 17.00, 18.30, 20.00 Tues–Sun, July & Aug; 12.30, 14.00, 15.30, 17.00 Sat & Sun, March, Nov & Dec ⓝ Metro to Stadhuis; tram: 21, 23. Admission charge

SS *Rotterdam*

Once the flagship of the historic Holland-America Line, the SS *Rotterdam* is the largest passenger ship ever built in the Netherlands. On board are various bars, restaurants and shops, a theatre, hotel and conference facilities. ⓐ Katendrechtse Hoofd ⓣ (010) 484 0727 ⓦ www.derotterdam.com ⓝ Metro to Rijnhaven; bus: 77. Admission charge

Strand aan de Maas (Beach on the Maas)

From the end of May until the end of September, Rotterdam's superb 'urban beach' – replete with sand – sets up along the waterfront. A lounge atmosphere is enhanced by huge cushions, cocktails and inspired food. There's also a regular programme of live music and parties. ⓐ At the foot of Erasmus Bridge ⓣ (06) 20 51 16 28 ⓦ www.strandaandemaas.info ⓝ Metro to Leuvehaven; tram: 8, 20, 23, 25

Tropicana

An amazing, subtropical indoor water park (see page 35).

Walk of Fame

Rotterdam's answer to the Hollywood Walk of Fame. Those who have left their hand- or footprints in the concrete along this stretch include Shirley Bassey, Barry White and Katie Melua. ⓐ Schiedamsedijk ⓣ (010) 458 1694 ⓦ www.walkoffame.nl ⓛ 24 hours Ⓝ Metro to Beurs or Leuvehaven; tram: 8, 20, 23, 25

De Verwoeste Stad

This bronze work of art was created by Russian sculptor Ossip Zadkine and is Rotterdam's main war memorial. Entitled *The Devastated City*, it depicts a desperate figure of a man with no heart, powerfully symbolising the heart of the city which was ripped out during the 1940 bombardment. ⓐ Plein 1940 Ⓝ Metro to Beurs; tram: 8, 20, 21, 23, 25. Admission charge

Het Zakkendragershuisje (The Sack Carriers' House)

Dating from 1653, this house in the Delfshaven belonged to a guild responsible for carrying sacks of grain from the ships to the warehouses and distilleries. The last zakkendragers left in 1943 to work at the Van Nelle Factory. ⓐ Voorstraat 13–15 Ⓝ Metro to Delfshaven; tram: 4, 8

CULTURE

De Dubbelde Palmboom (The History Museum)

Within the Delfshaven and housed in a restored grain warehouse, this museum focuses on the city's trade through the ages. As well as examples of early advertising, interiors of old shops have been recreated. A large section is devoted to local hero, Piet Hein, who

was born in the Delfshaven. ⓐ Voorhaven 12 ⓣ (010) 476 1533
ⓦ www.dedubbeldepalmboom.nl ⓛ 11.00–17.00 Tues–Sun,
closed Mon ⓜ Metro to Delfshaven; tram: 4, 8. Admission charge

Het Havenmuseum (The Harbour Museum)

The Harbour Museum is a free-entry 'working' museum which
recreates the atmosphere of an operational harbour. It extends
outdoors where you can watch restoration work on all sorts of
vessels in the Leuvehaven and nearby Oude Haven (Old Harbour).
ⓐ Leuvehaven 50 ⓣ (010) 404 8072 ⓦ www.havenmuseum.nl
ⓛ 10.00–17.00 Tues–Fri, 11.00–17.00 Sat & Sun, closed Mon
ⓜ Metro to Beurs or Leuvehaven; tram: 8, 20, 21, 23, 25

⬥ The operational harbour of the Havenmuseum

Maritiem Museum (Maritime Museum)

The history of Rotterdam harbour comes to life at this museum, which stages exciting temporary exhibitions and houses around half-a-million nautical artefacts. Highlights include an interactive children's exhibition and a visit on board the *Buffel*, a 19th-century warship moored outside. ⓐ Leuvehaven 1 ⓣ (010) 413 2680 ⓦ www.maritiemmuseum.nl ⓛ 10.00–17.00 Tues–Sat, 11.00–17.00 Sun, Sept–June; 10.00–17.00 Mon–Sat, 11.00–17.00 Sun, July & Aug ⓜ Metro to Beurs; tram: 8, 20, 21, 23, 25. Admission charge

Nederlands Fotomuseum

The Dutch Photo Museum relocated from the Witte de Withstraat to the refurbished Las Palmas building on the Kop van Zuid in spring 2007. Its semi-permanent collection and temporary exhibitions focus on Dutch photography. ⓐ Wilhelminakade 332 ⓣ (010) 203 0405 ⓦ www.nederlandsfotomuseum.nl ⓛ 10.00–17.00 Tues–Fri, 11.00-17.00 Sat & Sun, closed Mon ⓜ Metro to Wilhelminaplein; tram: 20, 23, 25. Admission charge

Museum Pablo Rueda Lara

A small but fascinating museum dedicated to Rotterdam-based Spanish ceramist Pablo Rueda Lara (1945–1993). He was on the verge of moving to this charming building in the Delfshaven when he died. The ground floor exhibits his extraordinary, kitsch work which ranges from a crumpled Pepsi can to irreverent Pope mobiles. ⓐ Aelbrechtskolk 10 ⓣ (010) 476 0283 ⓦ www.pabloruedalara.com ⓛ 13.00–17.00 Sat & Sun, closed Mon–Fri ⓜ Metro to Delfshaven; tram: 4, 8

WORM

A hotbed of creativity and experimentation, WORM is an international underground platform for art, performance, movies and music (expect anything from improv and avant-rock to punk and electronica). The film programme soaks up obscure genres, cult classics and seldom-screened documentaries. ⓐ Achterhaven 148 ⓣ (010) 476 7832 ⓦ www.wormweb.nl ⓛ Times vary ⓜ Metro to Delfshaven; tram: 4, 8

RETAIL THERAPY

This area isn't terrifically big on shops: head straight indoors to the sumptuous Westelijk Handelsterrein for the cream of the crop.

Westelijk Handelsterrein (Western Trade Terrain) Thirty-six beautifully restored warehouses converge under a glass roof dating from 1894, and the vast space, with an upper and lower level, now houses luxury art galleries, restaurants and designer shops. Here you'll find Van Oosterom, the pilot store for Marcel Wander's fabulous Moooi range. In the evening, trendy establishments such as lounge bar-restaurant De Loft, wine bar En Verre and celebrity chef Herman den Blijker's romantic Italian restaurant Rosso draw a monied crowd. ⓐ Van Vollenhovenstraat 15 ⓛ Times vary ⓜ Metro to Leuvehaven; tram: 7, 20, 23, 25

TAKING A BREAK

Hotel New York £–££ ❶ The restaurant of this famous hotel is Rotterdam's ultimate dining experience. Amazingly, however, the prices suit all pockets and even the fussiest of palates will be assuaged by the extensive menu – and seafood lovers will delight in the Oyster Bar. ⓐ Koninginnenhoofd 1 ⓣ (010) 439 0525 ⓦ www.hotelnewyork.nl ⓛ 10.00–23.00 ⓝ Metro to Wilhelminaplein; tram: 20, 23, 25

▲ Dining in the ballroom of the Hotel New York

Loos £–£££ ❷ A popular, Parisian-style art deco establishment that has a smart restaurant and relaxed café. ⓐ Westplein 1 ① (010) 411 7723 ⓦ www.loos-rotterdam.nl ⓛ 09.00–01.00 Mon–Thur, 09.00–02.00 Fri–Sun Ⓝ Metro to Leuvehaven; tram: 7, 20, 23, 25

Z&M £–£££ ❸ The delicatessen serves fresh seasonal products, cheese, pasta, olive oil and organic meat, plus delicious sandwiches, quiches and tarts to take away. There's also a wine store with an eclectic choice of organic French wines, grappa and calvados. If you want to stay and graze, head upstairs to the unfussy, rustic-style restaurant with its charming terrace overlooking the River Maas. ⓐ Veerhaven 13 ① (010) 280 0980 ⓦ www.zenmdelicatessen.nl ⓛ 10.00–24.00 Mon–Sat, 11.00–24.00 Sun Ⓝ Metro to Leuvehaven; tram: 7, 20, 23, 25

AFTER DARK

RESTAURANTS

Abrikoos £££ ❹ This fantastic Mediterranean restaurant in the Delfshaven produces a great choice of tapas and never fails to create a warm, convivial atmosphere. ⓐ Aelbrechtskolk 51 (off Voorhaven) ① (010) 477 4140 ⓦ www.abrikoos.nl ⓛ 17.00–22.00 Mon–Thur, 17.00–23.00 Fri & Sat, 16.00–22.00 Sun Ⓝ Metro to Delfshaven; tram: 4, 8

Blits ££–£££ ❺ Dutch designer Marcel Wanders drew inspiration for the chic interior of this hotspot from the world of theatre.

Ceiling-to-floor windows guarantee stunning views over the River Maas, and its colourful terrace attracts a trendy crowd. The menu consists of 18 small dishes inspired by Japanese, North African and South American cuisine. Reserve the private 'Love-Suite' with its heart-shaped chairs and other romantic trappings for the ultimate in culinary coupledom. ⓐ Boompjes 701 ① (010) 282 9051 ⓦ www.blits-rotterdam.nl ⓝ NS/Metro to Blaak; metro to Leuvehaven; tram: 8, 20, 21, 23, 25 ① Note that this restaurant only opens for group bookings and private functions. Reservations essential

Fabbrica ££–£££ ⓺ A quirky, artistic Italian restaurant within an old factory. It specialises in pizza served from a huge wooden oven. Try and snag one of the three 'train compartments'. ⓐ Vijf Werelddelen 107 (Unit 12) ① (010) 485 7314 ⓦ www.fabbrica.nl ⓛ 12.00–14.30, 17.00–22.00 Mon–Fri, 17.00–22.00 Sat & Sun ⓝ Metro to Wilhelminaplein; tram: 20, 23, 25

Gaucho aan de Maas ££–£££ ⓻ A magnet for carnivores, this modern, upmarket grill restaurant has an enormous wooden terrace with stunning vistas across the River Maas. ⓐ Holland Amerikakade 900 ① (010) 484 5521 ⓦ www.gauchos.nl ⓛ 17.00–23.30 ⓝ Metro to Wilhelminaplein; tram: 20, 23, 25

Parkzicht ££–£££ ⓼ A stylish, yet comparatively inexpensive, bar-restaurant within Het Park. Try their high tea or pick up a picnic hamper to enjoy in the park. ⓐ Kievitslaan 25 ① (010) 436 8888 ⓦ www.parkzichtrotterdam.nl ⓛ 10.00–17.00 Mon & Tues, 10.00–01.00 Wed–Sun ⓝ Tram: 8

△ *Great views on offer at Blits*

Parkheuvel £££ ❾ On the edge of Het Park, Rotterdam's most exclusive restaurant – and one of the best in the Netherlands – is a gourmand's paradise. ⓐ Heuvellaan 21 ⓣ (010) 436 0530 ⓦ www.parkheuvel.nl ⓛ 12.00–14.30, 18.30–22.00 Mon–Fri, 18.30–22.00 Sat, closed Sun ⓝ Tram: 8

Wijn of Water £££ ❿ Patronised by creative and media types, 'Wine or Water' is unusually located within nine former sea containers on the Lloyd Pier. A 'multimedia restaurant', it boasts an interactive wine rack, audio-visual projections and a wireless network. The menu is Mediterranean, infused with Eastern influences. ⓐ Loods Celebs 101 ⓣ (010) 477 8454 ⓦ www.wijnofwater.nl ⓛ 12.00–22.00 Tues–Sun, closed Mon ⓝ Tram: 8

BARS & CLUBS

Club Rotterdam An über-cool venue with a stylish cocktail bar, hi-tech club, French-style café-tabac and European-fusion restaurant with stunning views across the Maas. Wilhelminakade 699 ⓣ (010) 290 8442 ⓦ www.caferotterdam.nl ⓛ 11.30–22.00 Mon–Thur, 11.30–23.00 Fri & Sat, 09.30–22.00 Sun ⓜ Metro to Wilhelminaplein; tram: 20, 23, 25

Club Vie A painfully hip club that includes an Ibiza-style 'chillout' room, where regular Hed Kandi and MTV parties are held. ⓐ Maasboulevard 300 ⓣ (010) 280 0238 ⓦ www.clubvie.com ⓛ 23.00–04.00 Thur, 22.30–05.00 Fri & Sat, closed Mon–Wed ⓝ NS/Metro to Blaak; tram: 21

Maassilo This huge former grain silo draws a hip, urban crowd every weekend. ⓐ Maashaven zz 2 ⓣ (010) 476 2452 ⓦ www.maassilo.com ⓛ 23.00–06.00 Fri & Sat, closed Sun–Thur ⓝ Metro to Maashaven; tram: 2

Waterfront This alternative pop venue is a mecca for young musicians who make use of its café, rehearsal spaces and sound studio. ⓐ Boompjeskade 15 ⓣ (010) 201 0980 ⓦ www.waterfront.nl ⓛ 10.30–01.00 Mon–Wed, 10.30–03.00 Thur, 11.30–04.00 Fri & Sat, 11.30–01.00 Sun ⓝ NS/Metro to Blaak; tram: 21

● *Paleis Het Loo in Apeldoorn*

Amsterdam

Notorious for its red-light district and liberal drug laws, the Dutch capital's other charms are often overshadowed. Yet its cobweb of canals – home to around 2,500 houseboats – which wind through its beautifully preserved inner city of gabled buildings dating from the 16th century, has earned it the moniker 'Venice of the North'. And deservedly so. It has more canals than Venice, and is just as romantic. And, like its Italian counterpart, it is a rich cultural mecca. It's cosmopolitan, creative, has a vibrant nightlife and a bustling centre replete with the ubiquitous bicycles, trams, horse-drawn carriages, pedal-powered rickshaws and errant tuk-tuks. But it's best, and easily, explored on foot.

GETTING THERE

Amsterdam is 74 km (46 miles) northeast of Rotterdam and the journey takes around one hour by train. Every day, a direct service runs roughly five times an hour from Centraal Station. Check the timetable on ☎ 0900 9292 🕸 www.ns.nl

Driving to Amsterdam takes roughly the same amount of time as going by train. To plan your route, see 🕸 www.route.anwb.nl

SIGHTS & ATTRACTIONS

Further information on many of the sights and attractions listed here can be obtained at **VVV Amsterdam Tourist Board**

▶ *Venice of the North – houses along just one of the many canals*

Amsterdam & Apeldoorn

● *A boat trip is a great way to see Amsterdam*

(ⓐ Stationsplein 10 ⓣ (020) 551 2525 ⓦ www.vvvamsterdam.nl
ⓛ 09.00–18.00 Mon–Sat, 09.00–17.00 Sun), whose main office
is opposite Centraal Station

Amsterdamse Historish Museum

This superb museum chronicles the history of the city through
engaging exhibitions. ⓐ Kalverstraat 92 ⓣ (020) 523 1822
ⓦ www.ahm.nl ⓛ 10.00–1700 Mon–Fri, 11.00–17.00 Sat & Sun
ⓝ Tram: 1, 2, 4, 5, 9, 14. Admission charge

Anne Frank Huis

The former hiding place of Anne Frank, and where she wrote her famous diary (the original is on display). ⓐ Prinsengracht 267 ⓣ (020) 556 7105 ⓦ www.annefrank.org ⓛ 09.00–19.00 mid-Sept–mid-March; 09.00–21.00 Mon–Fri & Sun, 09.00–22.00 Sat, mid-Mar–mid-Sept ⓝ Tram: 13, 14, 17 ⓘ go in the evening to avoid queues. Admission charge

De Begijnhof

This secluded *hofje* (hidden courtyard) originally served as a sanctuary for the Beguines, a religious sisterhood of unmarried women. An absolute treasure is its hidden Catholic church dating from 1665 (concealed behind the façade of a house). At number 34 is a wooden house dating from 1477, the oldest house in the city, plus the English Reformed Church built in 1495. Inside on the pulpit are four panels designed by a young Mondriaan. ⓐ Gedempte Begijnensloot, off Spui ⓦ www.begijnhofamsterdam.nl ⓛ 13.00–18.30 Mon, 09.00–18.30 Tues–Fri, 09.00–18.00 Sat & Sun ⓝ Tram: 1, 2, 5

Boat Trips

Several boat companies offer tours of the city but for something more intimate, try the non-profit St Nicolaas Small Boat Tours. Phone to reserve. ⓐ Meeting point: Boom Chicago Bar, Leidseplein 12 ⓣ (06) 50 80 53 48 ⓦ www.amsterdamboatclub.com ⓝ Tram: 1, 2, 5, 6, 7

Eastern Docklands

For centuries, the city of Amsterdam has remained virtually unchanged. However, over the past few years, the waterfront

to the east of its Centraal Station has undergone a remarkable renaissance. Here, among a mish-mash of gentrified warehouses, higgledy-piggledy buildings and eccentric bridges, celebrated Dutch and international architects have given the area a nautical touch. Head to architecture centre, **ARCAM** (ⓐ Prins Hendrikkade 600 ⓣ (020) 620 4878 ⓦ www.arcam.nl ⓜ Metro: Nieuwmarkt), for a detailed map of this wonderful area.

Pathé Tuschinski

One of the world's most beautiful cinemas, the Tuschinski opened in 1921 and is a breathtaking jumble of art deco, art nouveau and Amsterdam School. It screens all the latest blockbusters and is a magnificent place to hole up on a rainy day: book a box with champagne for a special treat. ⓐ Reguliersbreestraat 26–28 ⓣ 0900 1458 ⓦ www.pathe.nl ⓝ Tram: 1, 2, 5, 6, 7

TunFun

A gigantic indoor children's playground and café within a disused tunnel below a roundabout. ⓐ Mr Visserplein 7 ⓣ (020) 689 4300 ⓦ www.tunfun.nl ⓒ 10.00–18.00 (ticket desk shuts at 17.00) ⓝ Tram: 4, 9, 14. Admission charge

CULTURE

Foam

The city's leading museum for contemporary photography. ⓐ Keizersgracht 609 ⓣ (020) 551 6500 ⓦ www.foam.nl ⓒ 10.00–18.00 Mon–Wed, Sat & Sun, 10.00–21.00 Thur & Fri ⓝ Tram: 16, 24, 25. Admission charge

WHAT'S ON?

For information on events, including parties, visit ⓦ www.iamsterdam.com or pick up a free copy of English-language newspaper *Amsterdam Weekly*, also downloadable from ⓦ www.amsterdamweekly.nl

For tickets to, and info on, all cultural events, visit **AUB** (ⓐ Leidseplein 26 ⓣ 0900 0191 ⓦ www.aub.nl ⓝ Tram: 1, 2, 5, 6, 7).

The AUB's Last-Minute Ticket Shop (ⓦ www.lastminute ticketshop.nl) often has great deals.

OBA (Public Library)

The city's newest library, nicknamed the 'Bieb', has a huge collection of English-language books, music, DVDs and free internet – plus a fantastic restaurant on the top floor. ⓐ Oosterdokskade 143 ⓣ (020) 523 0900 ⓦ www.oba.nl ⓛ 10.00–22.00 ⓝ Tram: 4, 9, 16, 24

Rijksmuseum

While most of the museum is closed for renovations until 2010, a choice selection from its impressive collection remains on display, including Rembrandt's magnum opus, *Nightwatch*. ⓐ Jan Luijkenstraat 1 ⓣ (020) 674 7000 ⓦ www.rijksmuseum.com ⓛ 09.00–18.00 Mon–Thur, Sat & Sun, 09.00–21.00 Fri ⓝ Tram: 2, 5, 12. Admission charge

Stedelijk Museum CS

The city's premier contemporary art museum is temporarily

housed in an old postal building until 2009. ⓐ Post CS
(2nd & 3rd Floor), Oosterdokskade 5 ⓣ (020) 573 2911
ⓦ www.stedelijk.nl ⓛ 10.00–18.00 ⓝ Tram: 2, 5, 12.
Admission charge

Van Gogh Museum

Around 200 paintings and 500 drawings by the tortured artist
are on view, alongside works by his contemporaries. ⓐ Paulus
Potterstraat 7 ⓣ (020) 570 5200 ⓦ www.vangoghmuseum.nl
ⓛ 10.00–18.00 Mon–Thurs, Sat & Sun, 10.00–22.00 Fri
ⓝ Tram: 2, 5, 12. Admission charge

JENEVER

Concocted by Dutch alchemist Sylvius de Bouve, who
infused juniper berries into distilled spirits in an attempt
to find a cure for kidney and stomach disorders, Jenever
(which comes from *jeneverbes*, meaning 'juniper berry'),
was a forerunner of gin and is unique to the Netherlands.
Traditionally, it was sampled at *proeflokalen* (tasting houses),
and the best in town is **Wynand Fockink** (ⓐ Pijlsteeg 31
ⓣ (020) 639 2695 ⓦ www.wynand-fockink.nl), which opens
every day of the year from 15.00–21.00. Not only can you taste
some 20 types of jenevers but around 50 old Dutch liquors
with charming names such as 'Naked Belly Button' (originally
created for mums-to-be), 'Bridal Tears' (served after marriage
ceremonies) and 'Lotion of Venus' (reputedly an aphrodisiac).

RETAIL THERAPY

Amsterdam is fantastic for shopping. The main shopping route, the pedestrianised Nieuwendijk which leads into the Kalverstraat, starts just opposite Centraal Station and winds its way up, via Dam square, to the Singel Flower Market (and indoor shopping centre, the Kalvertoren). To avoid the crowds head off the beaten track to the Negen Straatjes (Nine Streets) or the Jordaan district to savour unique speciality shops and boutiques. Burgeoning shopping street, Haarlemmerstraat, is where you can find retail gems and delightful eateries among its otherwise touristy fare. The PC Hooftstraat, behind the Museumplein, is the city's most expensive retail area. While, by contrast, the city's famous flea market is at Waterlooplein and Amsterdam's largest general market runs the length of the Albert Cuypmarkt.

TAKING A BREAK & AFTER DARK

Latei £ A unique café-cum-kitsch bric-à-brac shop, just off the Nieuwmarkt square. Delicious for healthy breakfasts and lunches or afternoon tea with home-made apple pie and chocolate cake. ⓐ Zeedijk 143 ⓣ (020) 625 7485 ⓦ www.latei.net ⓛ 08.00–18.00 Mon–Sat, 11.00–18.00 Sun ⓜ Metro: Nieumarkt

De Bolhoed £–££ A charming vegetarian restaurant with a picturesque canalside terrace, just a short stroll from the Anne Frank Huis (see page 109). ⓐ Prinsengracht 60–62 ⓣ (020) 626 1803 ⓛ 12.00–22.00 ⓜ Metro: Prinsengracht

De Kas ££–£££ A white-linen organic restaurant within a 1926 greenhouse. Many of the ingredients are picked fresh from their own nursery. For an extra experience reserve the chef's table in the kitchen. Kamerlingh Onneslaan 3 (020) 462 4562 www.restaurantdekas.nl 12.00–14.00, 18.30–22.00 Mon–Fri, 18.30–22.00 Sat Tram: 9

Supperclub £££ Recline on mattresses while grazing on culinary delights served on platters from the open kitchen. In summer, the concept is extended to the Supperclub Cruise. Jonge Roelensteeg 21 (020) 344 6400 www.supperclub.com 19.30–01.00 Mon–Thurs & Sun, 19.30–03.00 Fri & Sat Tram: 1, 2, 4, 5, 13

ACCOMMODATION

Qbic Amsterdam WTC £ No-frills, affordable designer accommodation in a 'Cubi', a state-of-the-art cube-shaped space featuring mood lighting, a Hästens bed and bathroom fittings by Philip Starck. WTC, Strawinskylaan 241 (043) 321 1111 www.qbichotels.com

Amstel Botel £–££ A floating 3-star hotel on a ferryboat moored in a picturesque harbour a short walk from Centraal Station. Oosterdokskade 2–4 (020) 626 4247 www.amstelbotel.nl Tram: 4, 9, 14

Winston Hotel £–££ An inexpensive 'art hotel' bordering the Red Light District, with individually designed rooms and a lounge bar

● *Enjoy the luxury of a 5-star room at the Lloyd Hotel*

and small club attached. ⓐ Warmoesstraat 129 ⓣ (020) 623 1380
ⓦ www.winston.nl ⓝ Tram: 1, 2, 5

Lloyd Hotel £–£££ Dating from 1920, this art deco hotel within
the Eastern Docklands was originally built for Jewish immigrants
awaiting passage to America. Its individually designed 1- to 5-star
rooms are a showcase of Dutch architecture and design. ⓐ Oostelijke
Handelskade 34 ⓣ (020) 561 3636 ⓦ www.lloydhotel.com ⓝ Tram: 26

The Dylan Amsterdam £££ An exquisite boutique hotel
and a favourite haunt of the famous. ⓐ Keizersgracht 384
ⓣ (020) 530 2010 ⓦ www.dylanamsterdam.com ⓝ Tram: 1, 2, 5

Apeldoorn

Apeldoorn lies within Gelderland, the largest, and least populated, province in the Netherlands, which runs from the middle of the country to the east, bordering Germany.

With its verdant neighbourhoods and rigid, green infrastructure policy, the 'garden city of the Netherlands' is definitely the heart of the Veluwe, the country's 'green belt'.

It's within this region that the Dutch Royal Family chose, in the 17th century, to build their country estate, Paleis Het Loo (see page 118), a veritable *tour de force* of Dutch architecture, interior design and landscape gardening.

This area, with its vast nature reserves, is ideal to explore if you're a nature lover or if you simply feel like soaking up a great antidote to hectic city life.

GETTING THERE

Apeldoorn is 124 km (77 miles) east of Rotterdam, and takes approximately 90 minutes to reach by train. A service runs twice each hour every day from Centraal Station, and there are direct trains to Apeldoorn. Check the timetable (⊕ 0900 9292 ⓦ www.ns.nl).

If you drive to Apeldoorn, it will take roughly the same amount of time to get there as it does by rail, but do break up your journey in the medieval city of Utrecht, which is approximately half way. To plan your route, see ⓦ www.route.anwb.nl

▶ *The a-maze-ing gardens at Paleis Het Loo*

PALEIS HET LOO

Let Paris have Versailles; Apeldoorn has Paleis Het Loo. The Loo (pronounced 'Low') Palace is a magnificent, 17th-century country palace with sumptuous baroque parterre gardens, complete with fountains, statues and pergolas. It was the summer residence of the Dutch Royal Family from 1686–1975. Room after lavish room offers a glimpse into three centuries' worth of extravagant Dutch furnishing and interior styles, and contain a wealth of paintings, silver, china, royal garments and court costumes. Classical music concerts (🔘 www.paleisconcerten.nl) take place here every last Friday of the month except July and August. 🅰 Koninklijk Park 1 📞 (055) 577 2400 🔘 www.paleishetloo.nl 🕐 10.00–17.00 Tues–Sun, closed Mon 🛈 guided tours in English must be booked in advance. Admission charge

SIGHTS & ATTRACTIONS

Further information on many of the sights, attractions and events listed here can be obtained from **VVV Apeldoorn Tourist Board** (🅰 Deventerstraat 18 📞 (055) 526 0200 🔘 www.vvvapeldoorn.nl 🕐 09.00–18.00 Mon–Fri, 09.00–17.00 Sat, closed Sun).

Het Aardhuis

On the grounds of Paleis Het Loo (see above) and within a wildlife park, this house was built in 1861 by King Willem III as a place for the military to hold meetings. After his death in 1890, it became the royal hunting lodge and now serves as a museum, crammed with historical furniture and paintings. ⓐ Aardhuis 1, Hoog Soeren ⓣ (055) 519 1337 ⓦ www.aardhuis.nl ⓛ 10.00–17.00 Apr–Oct. Admission charge

Apenheul

This revolutionary monkey park allows almost 30 different species of primates, including bonobos, gibbons, orang-utans and gorillas, to roam freely in this huge wooded area; some even frolic among the visitors (don't be surprised to be greeted by squirrel monkeys climbing all over you). And don't worry: the less 'sociable' primates, such as gorillas, are on islands surrounded by a moat, so it's

● *A black-headed squirrel monkey at Apenheul*

very safe. Two per cent of revenue from the park is reinvested in education and (in situ) nature conservation. ⓐ JC Wilslaan 21–31 ⓣ (055) 357 5757 ⓦ www.apenheul.com ⓛ 09.30–17.00 Apr–June & Sept–Oct; 09.30–18.00 July & Aug ⓘ ensure you put all your valuables in one of the 'monkey-proof' bags provided at the entrance. Admission charge

De Hoge Veluwe

This vast national park of forest and sandy dunes is inhabited by rabbits, deer and other wildlife. Explore its 42 km (26 miles) of cycle paths on one of the many white bikes which are free to use. They can be picked up from one of the park's three entrances (Houtkampweg 13 in Hoenderloo, Houtkampweg 9 in Otterloo and Koningsweg 17 at Schaarsbergen). There are also special bikes for wheelchair users and tricycles for people with disabilities. It's great for picnics or simply for getting up close and personal with nature, but don't miss its rare treasures, which include the Kroller-Müller Museum (see page 122) and Jachthuis St Hubertus, a hunting lodge designed by H P Berlage. ⓐ Office address: Apeldoornseweg 250, Hoenderloo ⓣ (055) 378 8116 ⓦ www.hogeveluwe.nl ⓛ 09.00–18.00 Jan–Mar, Nov & Dec; 08.00–20.00 Apr; 08.00–21.00 May & Aug; 08.00–22.00 June & July; 09.00–20.00 Sept; 09.00–19.00 Oct (last entry one hour before closing). Admission charge

Kinderparadijs Malkenschoten

A fun – the owners would say heavenly – children's park with goats, chickens, a fish pond, water pedalos and a candle maker. ⓐ Dubbelbeek 4 ⓣ (055) 533 2803 ⓦ www.kinderparadijs

malkenschoten.nl ⏱ 10.00–18.00 Mar–Oct; 10.00–17.00
Nov–Feb. Admission charge

Koningin Juliana Toren

This old-style amusement park (for children up to 16) has around
45 attractions, plus free coffee and tea. ⓐ Amersfoortseweg 35
ⓘ (055) 355 3265 ⓦ www.julianatoren.nl ⏱ 10.00–17.00 late
Mar–May, Sept & Oct; 10.00–17.30 June–Aug. Admission charge

Park Berg & Bos

Built in the 1930s as part of a project for the unemployed,
the park was the forerunner to Floriade, a spectacular event
showcasing garden design. It contains 250 hectares (618 acres)
of walking routes, wild swine, deer and a butterfly garden.
ⓐ JC Wilslaan 21 ⓘ (055) 355 3017 ⓦ www.parkbergenbos.nl
⏱ 09.00–16.30 Jan–Mar, Nov & Dec; 09.00–17.00 Apr–June,
Sept & Oct; 09.00–18.00 July & Aug. Admission charge

Veluwsche Stroomtrein Maatschappij

During the summer months, the Veluwe Steam Train Company
offers rides on its (mostly 1940s and 1950s) steam trains from
Apeldoorn to Dieren. ⓐ Dorpstraat 140, Beekbergen
ⓘ (055) 506 1989 ⓦ www.stoomtrein.org

CULTURE

CODA Museum

This 'cultural warehouse' is Apeldoorn's contemporary art museum
and holds regular international exhibitions. Also here is the

city's public library and archive centre. ⓐ Vosselmanstraat 299
ⓣ (055) 526 8400 ⓦ www.coda-apeldoorn.nl ⓛ 10.00–17.30 Tues,
Wed & Fri, 10.00–20.30 Thur, 10.00–17.00 Sat, 13.00–17.00 Sun,
closed Mon. Admission charge

Dragon Boat Festival
In June or July each year (two weeks before the summer holiday),
colourful Chinese dragon boats race down the Apeldoorn Canal
in a festival which encompasses Chinese cuisine, a children's
circus and puppetry. ⓦ www.drakenbootfestival.com

Harley Davidson Day
Every year on Whit Monday, around 1,500 'Harleys' roar into the
centre of Apeldoorn for a bikers' fest. ⓦ www.harleydagapeldoorn.nl

Jazz in the Woods
Every last Friday in May sees the heart of Apeldoorn transformed
when outdoor stages are set up at various locations for free jazz,
blues and pop music. ⓦ www.jazzinthewoods.nl

JT Apeldoorn (Tivoli)
The city's main cinema shows the latest movie releases in
their original language. ⓐ Nieuwstraat 381 ⓣ (055) 576 0434
ⓦ www.jt.nl ⓘ foreign films are subtitled in Dutch

Kroller-Müller Museum
Within the Hoge Veluwe National Park, this small museum
has a sublime collection of works by Van Gogh and a sculpture
garden featuring creations by Auguste Rodin, Henry Moore and

Barbara Hepworth. ⓐ Houtkampweg 6. Otterlo ⓣ (0318) 591 241 ⓦ www.kmm.nl ⓛ 10.00–17.00 Tues–Sun, closed Mon ⓘ the sculpture garden closes at 16.30. Admission charge

Orpheus

Apeldoorn's main theatre has a broad programme of modern dance, ballet, musicals, opera and (Dutch) plays, as well as quality international performances such as The Peking Acrobats, Ennio Marchetto and The Kransky Sisters. Outside is Orpheus, a piece by Russian sculptor Ossip Zadkine (who was responsible for Rotterdam's *The Devastated City*, see page 94). ⓐ Churchillplein 1 ⓣ 0900 123 0123 ⓦ www.orpheus.nl

Sand Sculptures

From mid-June to the beginning of September, the stunning creations of professional sand sculptors from all over the world are displayed in the Berg & Bos Park. ⓦ www.zandsculptuurapeldoorn.nl

Sunday Afternoon Concerts

Free concerts of anything from big band to folk music, classical music and choirs take place by the water in the city's Oranjepark. ⓦ www.muziektentapeldoorn.nl

RETAIL THERAPY

With all Rotterdam has to offer, Apeldoorn could prove a little disappointing. Shops here usually open around 11.00 on Monday and stay open until 21.00 on Thursday.

De Orangerie This modern indoor shopping centre is in the heart of Apeldoorn and has around 75 diverse stores that sell everything from books and sports equipment to toys, electronic goods and clothing. ⓐ 7311, WL Apeldoorn ⓦ www.winkelcentrumoranjerie.nl ⓛ 11.00–18.00 Mon, 09.30–18.00 Tues, Wed & Fri, 09.30–21.00 Thur, 09.00–17.00 Sat, closed Sun

TAKING A BREAK & AFTER DARK

Gijs & Katrien ££ An informal (yet sophisticated) restaurant, with a surprising, French-international menu and eclectic wine list, on the city's 'restaurant street'. ⓐ Van Kinsbergenstraat 4 ⓣ (055) 576 7484 ⓦ www.gijsenkatrien.nl ⓛ 17.00–22.00 Wed–Sun, closed Mon & Tues

Roma ££ Good quality, large portions of Italian fare are served up at this atmospheric establishment run by Sicilian owners. ⓐ Hoofdstraat 166 ⓣ (055) 521 378 ⓛ 17.00–23.00 Wed–Sun, closed Mon & Tues

Salalay ££–£££ A charming, child-friendly Thai restaurant that's fab for vegetarians and has authentic food and furniture. ⓐ Van Kinsbergenstraat 15 ⓣ (055) 522 4433 ⓦ www.salalay.nl ⓛ 16.30–22.30 Mon, Wed–Sun, closed Tues

De Brugwachter £££ A stylish restaurant located within a house where the operator of the nearby bridge used to live. It has a gorgeous garden terrace on its grounds. ⓐ Molenstraat-Centrum 625 ⓣ (055) 360 0696 ⓦ www.debrugwachter.nl ⓛ 17.00–22.00

Het Posthuis Uitbaterij £££ Since 1620 there has always been an inn at this spot; Paleis Het Loo (see page 118) was built next door to it. Today it's a smart restaurant that dates from the 1930s and has a pleasant outdoor terrace and excellent food. ⓐ Koningsstraat 1 ⓣ (055) 521 3997 ⓦ www.het-posthuis.nl ⓛ 12.00–22.00 Mon–Fri, 18.00–22.00 Sat, closed Sun

◔ The belltower on the roof of an old townhouse in Apeldoorn

ACCOMMODATION

Camping De Hoge Veluwe £ A campsite in the heart of this beautiful nature park (see page 120), with a restaurant, shop, indoor and outdoor swimming pools, plus volleyball, basketball and hockey facilities. ⓐ Houtkampweg 13 ⓣ 0900 464 3835 ⓦ www.hoogeveluwe.nl

Hampshire Hotel Apeldoorn £ A comfortable hotel sitting in one of the greenest districts of Apeldoorn, bordering woodland areas and within a kilometre (half-a-mile) of Paleis Het Loo (see page 118) and Apenheul (see page 119). ⓐ Soerenseweg 73 ⓣ (055) 355 4555 ⓦ www.hotelapeldoorn.nl

Stayokay Apeldoorn £ Within walking distance of Apenheul, this hostel has two-, three-, four-, six- and eight-person rooms, all with their own toilet and shower. ⓐ Asselsestraat 330 ⓣ (055) 355 3118 ⓦ www.stayokay.com

Bilderberg Hotel De Keizerskroon ££ A comfortable, modern 4-star hotel opposite Paleis Het Loo. It has an indoor pool, sauna, solarium and Wi-Fi. ⓐ Koningstraat 7 ⓣ (055) 521 7744 ⓦ www.bilderberg.nl

Van der Valk Hotel De Cantharel ££ A large motel-style hotel (part of the Van der Valk chain), with a superb restaurant just outside Apeldoorn. ⓐ Van Golsteinlaan 20 ⓣ (055) 541 4455 ⓦ www.hoteldecantharel.nl

◑ *A river taxi speeds across the water*

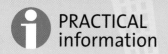

Directory

GETTING THERE

By air

Amsterdam's Schiphol Airport (see page 48) is the country's major airport and served by many UK and Irish airlines, including British Airways, BMI, EasyJet and Aer Lingus. There are 160 direct daily flights from the UK and flight time from London is 65–80 minutes.

Aer Lingus ☏ 0900 265 8207 ⓦ www.aerlingus.ie

BMI ☏ (020) 346 9211 ⓦ www.britishmidland.com

British Airways ☏ (020) 346 9559 ⓦ www.ba.com

EasyJet ☏ 0900 265 8020 ⓦ www.easyjet.com

KLM ☏ (020) 474 7747 ⓦ www.klm.com

Rotterdam Airport (see page 48) is served by fewer airlines flying to/from the UK – KLM Cityhopper, VLM Airlines and Transavia. However, you have the advantage of fast check-in procedures and arriving on the city's doorstep. The flight time from London is 50–85 minutes.

KLM Cityhopper ☏ (020) 649 9123 ⓦ www.klmcityhopper.com

Transavia ☏ 0900 0737 ⓦ www.transavia.com

VLM Airlines ☏ 0900 450 5050 ⓦ www.flyvlm.com

Visitors from elsewhere in Europe should travel via their nearest major city, all of which have plane and train connections to Rotterdam and/or Amsterdam.

Travellers from North America, Australia and New Zealand fly via Amsterdam. However, if you don't mind adding a day to your trip and fancy travelling to Rotterdam via Liverpool Street train station in London, and then direct by ferry (all Wi-Fi'd up, by the way), the Dutchflyer ticket (see ⓦ www.dutchflyer.co.uk) is a seductive option.

Many people are aware that air travel emits CO_2 which contributes to climate change. You may be interested in the possibility of lessening the environmental impact of your flight through Climate Care, which offsets your CO_2 emissions by funding environmental projects around the world. Visit ⓦ www.climatecare.org

By rail

Eurostar services to Brussels allow an onward connection direct to Rotterdam, with a total journey time of about five hours from the UK. The new NS (Dutch Railways) Hispeed train cuts times even more.

◔ *Reflections in glass at Rotterdam Centraal Station*

Eurostar ☎ (08705) 186 186 Ⓦ www.eurostar.com

NS Hispeed trains in the Netherlands Ⓦ www.nshispeed.nl

NS International for international trains ☎ 0900 9296
Ⓦ www.nsinternational.nl

OV Reisinformatie for all public transport in the Netherlands
☎ 0900 9292 Ⓦ www.9292ov.nl

Thomas Cook European Rail Timetable ☎ (01733) 416 477
Ⓦ www.thomascookpublishing.com

By road

There are ferry services (see below) or the Eurotunnel if you
wish to take your car to Rotterdam. Information on traffic is
available from the **ANWB** (Dutch AA) ☎ 0900 9622 (travel
information)/0800-0888 (breakdowns) Ⓦ www.anwb.nl

Eurolines is Europe's largest coach operator and travels from
London to eight cities in the Netherlands, including Rotterdam
and Amsterdam.

Eurolines ☎ (08705) 808080 Ⓦ www.eurolines.com

By water

Stena Line Superferries cross from Harwich to the Hook of
Holland in a journey time of 6 hours and 15 minutes. ☎ (08705)
707 070 Ⓦ www.stenaline.co.uk

P&O Ferries travel overnight from Hull to Rotterdam; the
journey takes 14 hours. ☎ (08705) 980 333 Ⓦ www.poferries.com

The Dutch Flyer is a 'rail and sail' service from London Liverpool
St (or connections in East Anglia) to any Dutch city. ☎ (08705)
455 455 Ⓦ www.dutchflyer.co.uk

ENTRY FORMALITIES

EU citizens can travel to the Netherlands without a visa. For citizens of the USA, Canada, Australia, New Zealand and South Africa, stays of up to 90 days do not require a visa. Visitors from other countries will require a visa. A valid passport is necessary.

EU citizens may bring personal possessions and goods for personal use into the Netherlands, provided they have been bought in the EU. However, if you are travelling from a country outside the EU, you can only bring in limited quantities free of tax. For full regulations check Ⓦ www.douane.nl

MONEY

The currency of the Netherlands is the euro (€), divided into 100 cents (also called eurocents). Notes are in denominations of €5, €10, €20, €50, €100, €200, €500; coins in €1 and €2 and cents worth 1c, 2c, 5c, 10c, 20c and 50c. Note, however, that many establishments won't take notes larger than €100. For current exchange rates, check Ⓦ www.travelex.com or Ⓦ www.oanda.com

ATMs (*geldautomaten*), banks and bureaux de change are dotted all over Rotterdam. Major international credit cards are accepted in most large stores (though generally not in supermarkets) and restaurants.

HEALTH, SAFETY & CRIME

Tap water is safe to drink and many public parks have drinking fountains.

Healthcare in the Netherlands is of a high standard and most doctors, nurses and paramedics are able to speak English.

Crime isn't a big issue in Rotterdam, but tourists are often targeted by pickpockets so use your common sense: always keep an eye on your valuables, particularly wallets, mobile phones and laptops – especially if you are on a tram. And be careful around the railway station, especially late at night.

OPENING HOURS

Shop opening hours vary but as a rule most are closed on Sunday (unless they're in the centre), and Monday morning. However, they open late until 21.00 on Friday.

Banks normally open 09.00–16.00 Monday to Friday, although some are open Saturday morning.

Museums are typically open from 10.00–17.00, but many are closed on Monday.

TOILETS

Public toilets are few and far between in Rotterdam. You may have to go to a café or restaurant if you suddenly get the call of nature (you will, however, be expected to buy a drink). Some toilets have attendants (particularly in clubs), who will expect a tip of at least 50 cents.

CHILDREN

Rotterdam isn't an especially child-friendly city, although small children are welcomed in most hotels, cafés and restaurants. To give them a taste of Rotterdam, take them to the Maritime Museum (see page 96), where there's a fun, interactive, nautical exhibition, and be sure to treat them to *pannekoeken* or *poffertjes* (types of pancakes) afterwards. Four to fourteen-year-olds can learn to make soap, develop photos, roast coffee or even milk a cow (albeit a fake one) at **De Ontdekhoek** (ⓐ Pannekoekstraat 55 ① (010) 414 3103 ⓦ www.ontdekhoed.nl), a fantastic kids' experimental centre. If any children still want to be engine drivers when they grow up, they should be shunted immediately to the enormous, interactive, indoor model railway at **Railz Miniworld** (ⓐ Ween 745 ① (010) 240 0501 ⓦ www.railzminiworld.com). It's hard to go wrong with a trip to the zoo, and Rotterdam's vast **Diergaarde Blijdorp** (ⓐ Blijdorpplaan 8 ① (010) 443 1495/1431 ⓦ www.diergaardeblijdorp.nl) boasts the Oceanium, with its underwater tunnel where sharks, turtles, stingrays and other marine life swim overhead. At the end of the day, put any tired little toddlers on the little 'train' that runs from the Oceanium back to the entrance. **Villa Zebra** (ⓐ Stieltjesstraat 21 ① (010) 241 1717 ⓦ www.villazebra.nl) is a children's museum which stages visual art exhibitions designed to stimulate creativity. And if you know any small people who need to expend some energy, make for **Plaswijckpark** (ⓐ Ringdijk 20 ① (010) 418 1836 ⓦ www.plaswijckpark.nl). Whether it's messing about on the water, go-karting, enjoying playground attractions or getting acquainted with wallabies and emus, this is one hectic hectare of pure fun.

COMMUNICATIONS
Internet

There are a number of internet cafés dotted around the city. If you have your own laptop head to the Orange flagship store (see page 70), which has free Wi-Fi.

easyInternetcafé ⓐ Stadhuisplein 16–18
Ⓦ www.easyeverything.com Ⓛ 09.00–23.00 Mon–Sat,
11.00–23.00 Sun Ⓜ Metro to Stadhuis; tram: 21, 23

Phone

Most public phone boxes take either credit cards or phone cards. You can buy a *telefoonkaart* (phone card) in post offices, tourist information centres and newsagents.

For **National Directory Enquiries**, call ☎ 0900 8008 and for **International Directory Enquiries**, call ☎ 0900 8418. To request a collect call from the Netherlands to a number abroad, call ☎ 0900 0101

TELEPHONING THE NETHERLANDS

The international dialling code for the Netherlands is 31. To dial any of the Dutch numbers in this book from your own country, dial your own international access code (00 from the UK), then 31, followed by the area code (leaving off the first 0), then the number. Most private homes in the Netherlands have seven digits.

TELEPHONING ABROAD

To dial abroad from the Netherlands, dial 00 followed by your own country's international code (UK 44, Ireland 353, USA and Canada 1, Australia 61, New Zealand 64, South Africa 27) and then the area code (leaving off the first 0) and number.

Post

There are plenty of post offices around the city. Rotterdam's main post office, however, has been shut down and replaced by a new concept – the *postwinkel* (post office shop) – with longer opening hours than a regular post office and queue-beating self-service facilities. What's especially fun for visitors is that you can print out postcards (and even stamps), directly from a USB stick or DVD, using your own photos.

TNT Postwinkel ⓐ Weena 296–298 ⓣ 0900 767 8526 (from NL only) ⓒ 09.00–18.00 Mon–Thur, 09.00–21.00 Fri, 09.00–17.00 Sat, closed Sun ⓝ NS/Metro to Centraal Station; tram: 4, 7, 8, 20, 21, 23, 25

Post boxes are easy to spot: they're red and marked with 'TNT Post' (they are being replaced with orange post boxes in 2009). The slot on the right is for local Rotterdam post; the slot on the left, marked *overige postcodes/bestemmingen* (other postcodes/destinations) is for post to the rest of the country or abroad.

ELECTRICITY

The Netherlands runs on 220 volts with two-pin continental plugs. British appliances will need an adapter; pick one up at the airport.

TRAVELLERS WITH DISABILITIES

If you are travelling to Rotterdam by train you can request assistance on your journey (and with help getting on and off the train). Contact the **Bureau Assistentieverlening Gehandicapten (Disabled Assistance Office)** (ⓣ (030) 230 235 7822) at least three hours before you start your journey. The platforms at Centraal

Station are all accessible by lift and there is a toilet for wheelchair users. All metro stations in Rotterdam have lifts, and metro trains have adequate access for wheelchair users. Generally speaking, the older trams aren't accessible for wheelchair users although these are being replaced by 'Citadis' trams which are accessible; they currently only run on line 20, 23 and 25. Most buses aren't accessible for wheelchairs. However, for the visually impaired, bus drivers or recorded messages will announce stops; the hearing impaired can see them on the LED display.

Accessible Rotterdam (ⓦ www.accessible.rotterdam.nl) offers general information for wheelchair users as well as accessibility of various buildings in the city.

TOURIST INFORMATION

The **Netherlands Tourist Board** is known as the Vereniging voor Vreemdelingenverkeer or VVV (ⓦ www.vvv.nl).

The **VVV Rotterdam Store** (ⓐ Coolsingel 5 ☎ 0900 403 4065 ⓦ www.rotterdam.info Ⓝ Metro to Stadhuis, tram: 21, 23) is the main tourist office in Rotterdam.

The **VVV Rotterdam Info Café** (ⓐ Café Engels, Stationsplein 45 ⏰ 09.00–17.30 Mon–Sat, 10.00–17.00 Sun Ⓝ NS/Metro to Centraal Station; tram: 4, 7, 8, 20, 21, 23, 25) is a handy offshoot of the tourist office, located right by Centraal Station where you can browse information with a cup of tea and cake.

Also located by the station is an alternative tourist information centre, **Rotterdam Use-it** (ⓐ Schaatsbaan 41–45 ☎ (010) 240 9158 ⓦ www.use-it.info Ⓝ NS/Metro to Centraal Station; Tram: 4, 7, 8, 20, 21, 23, 25), aimed at budget travellers.

BACKGROUND READING

The Adages of Erasmus by William Barker. Erasmus's fascinating collection of more than 4,000 proverbs, accompanied by his comments.

Architectural Guide to Rotterdam by Paul Groenendijk and Piet Vollaard. A comprehensive overview of the city's key buildings.

Erasmus and the Age of Reformation by Johan Huizinga. A biography of the Dutch writer and humanist, including his early years in Rotterdam.

The Last Jew of Rotterdam by Ernest Cassutto. The compelling true story of a Jew in hiding during German wartime occupation. The descriptions are vivid but its religious content might not be everyone's cup of tea.

The Praise of Folly by Desiderius Erasmus. Written in 1509, it's regarded as one of the most influential works in Western civilisation.

Rotterdam and the Sea: Four Centuries of Passenger Travel by Bram Oosterwijk. From the Pilgrim Fathers' departure from Delfshaven to today's profitable cruise trade.

Emergencies

Toll-free number for all emergencies (Ambulance/Fire/Police) 🕿 112
Call from any phone box, landline or mobile phone. There are
English-speaking operators 24 hours a day.

Lost property
Tram, Bus & Metro 🕿 (010) 447 6111 (phone after 14.00)
Rotterdam Airport 🕿 (010) 446 3450
Schiphol Airport 🕿 (020) 794 0800

MEDICAL SERVICES
Visitors from the UK require a European Health Insurance

EMERGENCY PHRASES

Fire!	**Help!**	**Stop!**
Brand!	Hulp!	Stop!
Brant!	*Hul-ep!*	*Stop!*

Call the fire brigade!	**Call the police!**
Waarschuw de brandweer!	Bel de politie!
Vaarskoow de brant-veer!	*Bel de pol-eet-see!*

Call an ambulance!
Waarschuw een ziekenauto!
Vaarskoow an zeeken-owtoe!

Card (EHIC), which guarantees emergency treatment. See ⓦ www.dh.gov.uk for more information.

Emergency doctors – Dokterstelefoon 📞 (010) 420 1100

Emergency dentist – Tandartsenlijn 📞 (010) 455 2155

Hospitals
Erasmus MC 🅰 's-Gravendijkwal 230 📞 (010) 463 9222
Havenziekenhuis 🅰 Haringvliet 2 📞 (010) 404 3300
IJsselland Ziekenhuis 🅰 Prins Constantijnweg 2 📞 (010) 258 5000

POLICE
In case of theft or a non-urgent emergency, head to the main 24-hour *politie* (police) headquarters (🅰 Doelwater 5 📞 0900 8844 (0800 8112 for the hearing impaired) Ⓜ Metro to Stadhuis; tram: 4, 7, 8, 20, 21, 23, 25).

EMBASSIES & CONSULATES
American Embassy 🅰 Lange Voorhout 102, The Hague 📞 (070) 310 9209
Australian Embassy 🅰 Carnegialaan 4, The Hague 📞 (070) 310 8200
British Embassy 🅰 Lange Voorhout 10, The Hague 📞 (070) 427 0427
Canadian Embassy 🅰 Sophialaan 7, The Hague 📞 (070) 311 1600
Irish Embassy 🅰 Dr Kuyperstraat 9, The Hague 📞 (070) 363 0993
New Zealand Embassy 🅰 Eisenhowerlaan 77-N, The Hague 📞 (070) 346 9324
South African Embassy 🅰 Wassenaarseweg 40, The Hague 📞 (070) 392 4501

A

Aanschouw 74
abseiling 34
accommodation 36–9
    Amsterdam 114–15
    Apeldoorn 126
air travel 48, 128–9
Ahoy 20
Alexandrium 25
Amsterdam 104–15
Amsterdamse Historisch
    Museum 108
Anne Frank Huis 109
Apeldoorn 116–27
Apenheul 119–20
Arboretum
    Trompenburg 35
architecture 20–1
art 20–2, 74, 79

B

bars & clubs see nightlife
Beach on the Maas 93
beer 27
Begijnhof 109
Berg & Bos Park 121
Beurs/WTC 58
Beurstraverse 24
Bibliotheek Rotterdam 62
Binnenrotte Market 25
boat accommodation 39
Boijmans van Beuningen
    Museum 78
books 137
bus travel 53

C

cafés
    Amsterdam 113–14
    Apeldoorn 124–5
    Centre 69–70
    Museumpark 82–3
    Waterfront 97–9
canal trips, Amsterdam 109
car hire 56
casino 33
Centraal Station 48
Central Rotterdam 58–73
Chabot Museum 74–8
City Hall 62–3
children 120–1, 132–3
chips 29
cinema 33, 63–4, 78, 110, 122
Cinerama Rotterdam 78
coach travel 49, 130
CODA Museum 121–2
crime 131, 139
culture 20–3
customs & duty 131
cycling 34, 53

D

dam 17, 39–3
dance 20
De Kooning, Willem 14
Delfshaven 87, 90
Delft 91
Delta Works 42
Desiderius Erasmus
    Statue 58
Diergaarde Blijdorp Zoo 133

disabilities 135–6
Doelen 63
Dragon Boat Festival 122
driving 49, 104, 116, 130
Dubbelde Palmboom 94

E

Eastern Docklands,
    Amsterdam 109–10
electricity 135
embassies &
    consulates 139
emergencies 138–9
entertainment 30–3
    see also nightlife
Erasmus 14
Erasmus Bridge 86–7, 92
Euromast 90–1
events 10–13, 45, 122

F

famous Rotterdammers
    14–15
ferries 130
festivals 10–13, 45, 122
Feyenoord Stadium 34
Foam Museum 110
food & drink 26–9
football 34

G

Groene Passage 67

H

Harbour Museum 95
harbour tours 56, 93
Harley Davidson Day 122

Havenmuseum 95
health 131
Het Aardhius 118–19
Het Park 90–1
Het Schielandshuis 64
Het Witte Huis 63
Het Zakkendragershuisje 94
history 16–17
History Museum 94–5
Hoge Veluwe 120
Holland-America Line 87–90
hospitals 139
Hotel New York 38, 97–8
hotels *see* accommodation
Huis Sonneveld 78–9

I
insurance 138–9
internet 133–4

J
Jazz in the Woods 122
Jenever 112
JT Apeldoorn (Tivoli) 122

K
Keukenhof 42
Kijk-Kubus 91
Kinderdijk Windmills 42
Kinderparadijs Malkenschoten 120–1
Koolhaas, Rem 14–15
Koopgoot 24
Kop van Zuid 87

Kroller-Müller Museum 122–3
Koningin Juliana Toren 121
Kunsthal Rotterdam 79

L
language 18, 24, 27, 49, 138
Lantaren/Venster 63–4
Leuvehaven 86, 95
lifestyle 18–19, 111
Lijnbaan 24
listings 32–3
Lloyd Quarter 87
lost property 138

M
Maas River 87–97
MAMA 79
Maritiem Museum 96
markets 25
metro 53–6
money 131
Museumpark 74–85
museums 20–2, 45
music 20, 30–3, 123

N
Natuurhistorisch Museum 80
Nederlands Architectuur Instituut 80
Nederlands Fotomuseum 96
nightlife 30–3
  Amsterdam 113–14
  Apeldoorn 124–5

Centre 72–3
Museumpark 84–5
Waterfront 102

O
OBA Library 111
Ontdekhoek 133
opening hours 132
Orpheus Theatre 123
Oude Haven 16, 86, 95

P
Pablo Rueda Lara Museum 96
Paleis Het Loo 118
Park Berg & Bos 121
parking 49
passports & visas 131
Pathé Schouwburgplein 64
Pathé Tuschinski 110
Pelgrimvaderskerk 91
phone 134
Pilgrim Fathers Church 91
Plaswijckpark 133
police 139
Poppentheater 45
post 135
public holidays 13
public transport 53

R
rail travel 48–9, 104, 116, 129–30
Railz Miniworld 133
restaurants 26–9
  Amsterdam 113–14

Apeldoorn 124–5
Centre 70–2
Museumpark 83–4
Waterfront 99–101
Rijksmuseum 111
Roodkapje 79
Rotterdam Library 62
Rotterdam Theatre 64
Rotterdam Welcome
Card 52

S
Sack Carriers' House 94
safety 131–2
sailing restaurants 29
St Laurens Church 58–62
Sand Sculptures 123
Scheepswerf 'De Delft' 91
Schielandshuis 64
Schouwburg 64
seasons 10
Shipping Quarter 86
shopping 24–5
Amsterdam 113
Apeldoorn 123–4

Centre 66–9
Museumpark 81–2
Waterfront 97
Show Cube 91
Skatepark Westblaak 74
sport & relaxation 34–5
SS Rotterdam 93
Stadhius 62–3
Station Blaak 63
Stedelijk Museum 111–2
Strand aan de Maas 93
swimming 35
symbols & abbreviations 6

T
taxis 56
TENT 81
theatre 20, 45, 64, 123
tickets 32–3
time difference 48
tipping 29
toilets 132
tourist information 104–8,
118, 136
tours 53, 56, 93, 109

trams 56
Tropicana 35
TunFun 110

V
Van Gogh Museum 112
Veluwe Steam Train
Company 121
Verwoeste Stad 94
Villa Zebra 133

W
Walk of Fame 94
water taxis 56, 90
Waterfront 86–103
weather 10, 46–7
Westelijk
Handelsterrein 97
White House 63
Witte de With Centrum
voor Hedendaagse
Kunst 81
WORM 97

Z
zoo 133
Zuidplein 25

Editorial/project management: Lisa Plumridge
Copy editor: Paul Hines
Layout/DTP: Alison Rayner
Proofreader: Wendy Janes